Sixty Single and Still Sizzling

Sixty Single and Still Sizzling

The Search for Mr. Right

Dawn La Puma

Copyright © 2024 Dawn La Puma
All rights reserved.

 A catalogue record for this book is available from the National Library of Australia

ISBN 978-0-6450329-2-5 (paperback)
ISBN 978-0-6450329-3-2 (e-book)

Cover Design: Janvi S Gajbhiye

Acknowledgements

I acknowledge my children who have encouraged and supported me along the road to Mr Right. They have listened, loved and given advise. They have laughed with me and upheld me as I despaired to ever get through the quagmire of dead ends. I also acknowledge my Mr Right who is with me all the way, wherever the road leads.

Table of Contents

About Me. 1
Why I am here on the Dating Scene at 64 Years Old

Getting Out and About. 6
Meeting People the Old-Fashioned Way

Dating Agencies. 9
Where You Only Meet Others Registered with the Dating Agency

Online Dating. 11
The Modern Way to Find a Partner

Setting up Your Profile. 14
The First Step on the Road to Mr Right

So, it Begins. 18
Trying to Sort the Good, The Bad and the Ugly and the Scammers.

Scammers 20
How to Recognise One or One Hundred.

Lists and More Lists. 23
The Rules of Engagement

More Lists 25
This time on Detecting Scammers.

First Meet Up. 28
When All the Work Comes to Fruition.

Ground Rules for Dating. 31
Make some Decisions Before you are Forced to.

The Elephant in the Room 37
When it is the Right Time to Have Sex

More Meet Ups 41
And More Dead Ends.

Things You Do for Love. 46
But Mostly the Things you Won't Do for Anything

Problems of a Different Kind. 53
Erectile Disfunction Raises its Head, (or not).

Don't Judge a Book by its Cover. 59
Or by the First Few Chapters

People Who come and Go 67
For One Reason or Another.

Sixty Single and Still Sizzling

Getting Things Mixed up. ········· **79**
It was Bound to Happen

Mr Right ········· **82**
The Story of You.

Conclusion. ········· **90**
Nearly Two Years of Being in Love and Being Loved

Dating Worksheet ········· **92**
My Rules
Do's and Don'ts
Dates and stories. What worked for me What didn't.
Names Address telephone Nos.
Sensitive Information.
Notes in case you too decide to write your memoirs.

About Me.

Why I am here on the Dating Scene at 64 Years Old.

A little background information about myself, and how I came to be on the dating sites and searching for my Mr Right.

I am an ordinary woman, a mother and a grandmother. I do not have a model figure nor a model face. I have worked since I was sixteen, born in the country where life is laid back and mostly friendly. I was a mature age university student and have a B.A. I am a visual Artist. My husband and I were running a gallery café in the country when everything changed. My husband had contracted pancreatic cancer, the silent killer, when we discovered its presence, it was advanced past the stage when we had any hope for a positive outcome. He passed away a few months after the initial diagnosis. Thus, I was widowed in my early sixties. This was a difficult period for me as I could no longer run the gallery alone as it was a small business and there was not enough income from it for staff. I was forced to sell my property and move away from the area. Everything would change. Where I lived, how I worked, all of this, and I would be doing it all alone. I did have the support of family and friends, but I had to go through all these changes as a single woman. Just as so many other people do when they lose a loved one. I had done this in my life once before and had not thought I would have to go through it again.

A few years after this I decided, for many reasons, that I would like to once again be in a relationship. I joined a dating site and I tried to get into a few different activities. I was a newcomer to the town where I now worked and lived, and it was not easy to make friends. Some of the activities that I had a go at were fun and some disastrous.

This book is an attempt to look at my experience, to enjoy a good laugh at myself and the places and people I met along the way. It is my strong desire that you too will see the funny, sad and many times hilarious sides to the stories I am going to relate. I trust that you will also get a sense of not being alone in this dating game, that others are walking, sometimes stumbling along, the same path and many, like me, have found the path which eventually led to their own true love. Certainly, in my case it did. I have family and friends who have met their partner this way so there is definitely room for hope.

The dating game can be compared to a circus and it's important to discover who is the ringmaster. Who are the performers and who just want to have the best seats in the audience. There are those who will stay till the end of the show and others who will only stay for the parts they like. This is maybe the ice cream and popcorn, perhaps, or the dancing horses. There are also the clowns, never underestimate the clowns and their ability to make you laugh, if you remember not to take their antics seriously. Some clowns use humour to hide a dark side to their personality. Then there are the highly strung trapeze artists, strutting around in their spangled costumes, showing off their prowess on the bars. All of this makes a delightful bright and apparently happy scene. But don't be fooled. Keep your eyes open and not just on the main arena.

I hope to make you aware of the dangers in online dating, to help you recognise a scammer and to decide for yourself if you want to play with the players or be tricked and manipulated into playing a game you won't or don't like.

Sixty Single and Still Sizzling

As I am a heterosexual female, almost all my stories involve men who may or may not have acted with integrity. In some cases, they have appeared to not have any sort of intelligence. I am astutely aware that there are women who can be described the same way. I have also been fortunate enough to meet a few gentlemen, who, despite us not being compatible in the dating side of life, I have become friends with, and we talk regularly. I have been blessed by some of these male friends sharing their experience with me so there is an attempt to address this gender imbalance and to look from the male point of view.

I really enjoy having male company, especially when it is someone you love, and they love you. I would not have put in the effort I did, over several years, into finding my perfect match. I feel I have written this book predominantly for women, but it is equally applicable to men searching for their perfect partner. One thing I have learned is that no two people are alike, and that men and women have a vast chasm filled with differences between them.

This book is about my own experiences and those of my friends and acquaintances. My reactions, my thoughts and feelings and emotions are all here on the paper. If here and there I sound frustrated, angry or totally disheartened then, at that point in time, I was exactly that. One day my friend, a lovely lady, finding me in tears after yet another failed attempt at finding Mr. Right said, and I quote, 'You will kiss a lot of frogs before you find Prince Charming,' This made me laugh and I have hung onto it when yet another froggy goes down the drain. I often wished I hadn't kissed them. Sometimes I was angry at myself for being an idiot and not seeing through the other person. Be ready to chastise yourself, forgive yourself, then take some deep breaths and get back in the game.

I do not profess to be an expert in dating and relationships, nor do I have any formal training in counselling or sexual disfunction or scammer detection. I'm simply telling you the story of my life during these very crazy, but always entertaining years.

Everything I've written about in these pages happened, if not to me then to some friends that have shared with me their own experiences. A few friends, both male and female, have added some of their own stories. I have used the stories and have mixed and matched them so that they are not easily recognised and thus I will give no hint of an identity of any participant in my story. All the names of men and women, and timeline of dates, have been deliberately changed as well. I have done this so that it will not be possible to figure out, and thus know, who did what to who. It is not my intention to hurt anyone so if you think a story is about you, it's probably not. If you can relate to it, then maybe you can contemplate on that and consider a change to your behaviour if necessary. Rest assured, however, everything written here is true.

My story is not a guidebook but maybe more of a 'heads up,' literally, to internet dating, staying safe, sane, and coming through relatively normal when dating in your sixties. It is all applicable at any age. I have discovered that laughter really is the best medicine, and you will laugh a lot in the search for Mr Right. Sometimes you will cry and sometimes you will be in despair as to what you are actually trying to achieve but in the end it's laughter that keeps you going.

I do not want my experiences to discourage or encourage you but to remind you that you are not alone. That we can talk about these topics without any feelings of guilt. My stories are a true and uncensored look at the sometimes disturbing, always hilarious, world of mature age dating and of course mature age sexuality.

Parts of the book are meant to give us an insight as to how the dating game and mature age sexuality works or doesn't work. It can be a lot of fun. Speed dating and online dating can be addictive, and it can also be depressing as you will find many dead ends. People won't answer you; you will be kind and answer someone's initial contact only to be told, 'sorry I'm not interested in you,' and this is from those that are courteous enough to bother to tell you this at all. Somewhere beyond all this negativity hides the very real possibility and hope of finding that diamond in the rough. Mr Right may be the next, 'Hi how are you?'

It is important for all of us to be safe, informed, and have some idea of what we are getting into when we decide it's time to stop taking matters in our own hands and get out there and find a partner who is also Mr Right.

Getting Out and About.

Meeting People the Old-Fashioned Way.

Before I get onto the online dating stuff, I wanted to say I did try traditional methods to, 'get out there' but they did not help, a couple of these occasions that I remember clearly are recorded here.

Perhaps one of my more unrealistic outings was an attempt to join a ladies darts team. I was asked 'do you play darts? to which I responded, 'no, never played and I'm not sure it's my scene as I'm a bit of a stay-at-home person and I can't remember the last time I stepped inside a pub.' I was reassured it was an all-ladies group and not much ever happened at the pub on Sunday night. Work tomorrow, was the reason given for that. I was keen on meeting some friends as my social life was zero, so I decided to face my fears and just do it.

Well, the first night I went along was the Sunday of a long weekend. The idea that the pub would be empty was not right as there was, 'no work tomorrow' for all the local lads, they all had the Monday off. The pub was full of raucous, drunken men, staggering on and off the dart floor. Some of the ladies gave them a talking to and it helped for a while. Finally, it was my turn to play and despite my best efforts I could barely hit the dart board with my borrowed darts. On my second shot one of the young men staggered onto the dart floor, I decided quickly he was a better target, as by now I was a bit over them being obnoxious. Now I did not throw directly at him, but he staggered across my line of sight, mid throw, and I did not stay my hand. Lucky for him I had little strength and the dart bounced off his chest. He didn't even register the hit and I got to retake the shot.

During one of the other team player's shots, I was apparently, 'Talking too loud,' and she gave me an evil snarl. Yes snarl! Serious game this darts. I couldn't wait to get out of there. By now the men were fighting and beer was all over the floor, broken glasses on the way to the bathrooms and all in all an appalling place to be. I was definitely, 'a fish out of water'. Above all of this was my embarrassment in the game itself. Neither me, or my opponent could peg out, and we reverted, after three attempts to peg out, to highest dart wins. Her dart hit the board but bounced back and onto the carpet. I did hit the board and my dart held long enough for me to be declared the winner. My first game of competition darts and I had won. Despite this amazing success I never went back, I was not asked again which was a big a relief to all involved.

I also joined a seniors games night to see if I could meet anyone, male or female, to be friends with. There were four people in attendance on the night I went along, and I was one of them. A lady in her seventies, a man my age who I had already met, and a man in his fifties who was known not be to the easiest person to get along with. I decided to go with the flow and just try to enjoy the evening. We played Pictionary on a white board, and we all had a good laugh when one man's drawing initially, resembled a penis which got the other three of us a little concerned as to where he was going. It was fun but the group ended soon after. Perhaps the drawings were too risqué.

During this time when I was trying to get out and about a friend kept prompting me that a certain gentleman that came into our shop often, was keen on me. I liked the man but as no interest, except friendliness, had been revealed to me I just ignored the idea that he liked me romantically. I had decided I would learn to play the harmonica and he was helping. One night at a music concert he arrived all dressed up and invited me to join him for a wine. My friend said, 'See I told you, but he won't make the first move, you will have to. Its how it is these days. Men do not know where they stand, they won't do anything.' So, with a lot of reluctance I asked, 'how would you like to go out for dinner one night?' He looked at me with a look of alarm on his face and said, 'I can't go out to dinner, I am about to have a hip replacement.' Luckily, I have a great sense of the ridiculous and I started laughing. I said, 'I'm asking you for dinner. Nothing else'. He then realised what he had said, and he started laughing as well. We had a fun night and months later he did ask me for lunch, but it was all too late by then.

Dating Agencies.

Where You Only Meet Others Registered with the Dating Agency.

I want to add a short paragraph here about more traditional dating agencies, and how it all appears to work. I have not engaged an agency myself and have little knowledge of how they work but, in this case, nothing was working in my girlfriend's favour. I also have a male friend who was an agency client for years. He never found his mate this way. Maybe other agencies may have done better for my female friend, I am simply telling her story. So, my female friend, in her early fifties, a lively, attractive and easy to get on with lady, decided not to get involved with the quagmire of online dating sites and sought out a dating agency to help her find true love. She supplied her details and a description of herself, a photograph of herself and a detailed description of who and what she would consider to be the perfect man for her.

After paying her money and waiting several weeks she was set up with her first date. She was not given any picture of her date just phone numbers were given to set up the meeting place. The man who showed up and introduced himself was in his seventies, lived with his children and quite obviously drank a bit too much. He was sozzled when she arrived. Now not all of this is bad. Well, the sozzled part is. But she had stipulated she was interested in men in the fifty to sixty years age group. She had also asked to be matched up with men on the same financial page as herself. This gentle man was not even in the same book. He was not even in the same section at the library. But worst of all he was a drunk. His facial features gave evidence to the fact he had not taken up drinking a few months ago. She told me he did not even appear that interested in the date but wanted to keep drinking.

When she talked to the proprietor of the dating agency to address the miscalculation and interpretation of her requests she was met with these answers. 'You are setting yourself too high. Men of fifty and sixty do not want to date women in their fifties. They are interested in much younger women. You will have to lower your expectation.'

She allowed herself to be persuaded into another date with a man in his late sixties, young at heart and a great outdoorsy type she was told. They forgot to tell her he couldn't speak two words unless one of them was an expletive. Most of these words were the sort you would hope your prospective man did not come out with on the first date. The man who showed up and introduced himself was, 'fucking amazed at how fucking gorgeous she was.' He hadn't fucking expected this. 'What the fuck. Wait till I tell my mates.'

She has kissed her money goodbye and doesn't even bother to communicate with the agency it is obvious that they are not listening to her, and she is being used by the agency to fulfil their, 'at least one date every three months,' policy.

Online Dating.

The Modern Way to Find a Partner.

An acquaintance of mine told me the only way to find a date in this age was online dating, 'Have a go, what have you got to lose?' were her exact words. My mind, my sanity, my time, were just a few of the things that would be sacrificed on the altar of computerized mate finding.

Online dating is not for the fainthearted. You need to have a thick skin, like a rhino. You need to be canny to weed out scammers. You must be determined and have a good memory not to mix up the lovely men, all of which are vying for your attention. You must also try to remember who is who, where they live and what their prospects are of being a match for you. I did not keep a notebook at the start of my quest, but looking back I wish I had. It would have helped in this endeavour to get it all on paper. Men were listed in my phone as, Phil Pinjarra, Don Donnybrook, and so on. This was helpful if they called but not if you had met two in one town and could not remember their names.

One of the skills I didn't have when I posted my first profile was telling people that I did not like their profiles and thus did not want to talk with them. I was taught to be polite. But in this situation, politeness is not always reciprocated, and it can waste a lot of your time.

Once you begin talking on the site with a man and you decide you don't want to continue, you must disengage. Best to not get started if you do not find them attractive to you. You will view endless pictures of middle-aged, older aged, men, who have no idea how to take a selfie. Men who take pictures of themselves in the mirror or worse still while they are driving and all you can see is nostril hair. Hopefully all this hair is up the nostrils, but this is not always the case. A meet up for coffee once confirmed that hair can grow pretty much anywhere. You must not melt with compassion when this happens. He really is an idiot and should know better.

I have learnt a great deal over the last few years, and I now think it would have been less confusing if I had been able to look at online profiles like I went clothing shopping. Or visited the library perhaps. If you are out to look for a new piece of clothing, say a new dress, you don't go into the shop and stare in amazement at every item. You disregard the jackets and coats; you walk past the trousers and jeans. You may admire a lovely cut or style or colour as you go bye, but it's not what you are here for, so you move on. Then once in the correct section of the store, you pay more attention and wait till something pops off the rack and catches your eye. You look at individual styles, colours and sizes, long or short skirts. You look where things are made, the cost, the cut, how does it fit you. You try on the dress, after time and consideration of all these different aspects of the purchase you decide, and the dress is yours. You take it home. Hopefully you don't discover it pulls under the arm or is too tight somewhere but at least you have been focused and have chosen the best way you could. You can take it back, if you haven't worn it.

Men could maybe use the analogy of purchasing a car. Perhaps. Before you get to the car yard, do your homework. Know what you are looking for. Know your spend limit. Check out all the aspects of a vehicle that interest you. Don't waste the salesman's time on things you know you won't buy, even if he offers deals too good to be true. Make sure you can afford what you choose and the maintenance which can be high in some types.

Setting up Your Profile.

The First Step on the Road to Mr Right.

Your profile is the first hurdle. We women agonise over what to write, we don't want to sound too eager, too boring, too forward, too slow, too fast. Too old or too young, too serious or too frivolous. We should not be too modern but not old fashioned. We must show that we are interested in a full relationship but not seem too ready to jump into bed with the first guy we meet.

It takes hours to answer these questions. Well at least the first time it does after that you're a little cannier and realise most men don't even read it at all and the ones that do read everything want a guitar playing, french cook, who is also skinny, with an athletic body and who enjoys deep sea diving and hiking and must love sex. Oh! If she can teach him French while he plays his mandolin, and she softly massages his back, all the better. She must be self-sufficient but not too independent. In other words, he's an idiot who you should scroll directly passed, having a quiet chuckle as you imagine him writing this crap and now, sitting at his computer, wondering why the only answers he has had are French scammers. Or any scammer with a word of French for that matter.

Sixty Single and Still Sizzling

Getting back to your profile, at the start of this process, you are really in earnest, so you think of every possible situation and answer honestly, even the body type question, I admit that at this mature age there are wrinkles and extra bits and pieces that were not jiggling around twenty years ago. You're not obese but you're not slim either. You don't want to, but you feel you must be truthful in your answer. If you do get passed all this administration stuff and connect with a real man, you must then eventually meet him. If you have been exaggerating about anything, and if the online conversation goes well and it all works out and you do get naked in front of him, he is going to notice. So, lying about your body type is not an option. Well not for you.

I met an Italian man who appeared to look great for his age. He truthfully said he was seventy years old. He had a great physique not thin but not overweight. When we met, he was an old man with a very big chubby belly and was not so healthy looking. The post was ten years ago at his son's wedding. He had not aged well.

So, you start thinking about this getting naked business, that leads to, 'do I really think I can have sex with an old man?' Hmm you're an old woman so why not, but how do you approach all of this and is it worth it and maybe you're better off as you are. The top drawer has been keeping everything sorted for a while now. Nothing in there requires more than an occasional recharge and now and again a replacement. You don't even need batteries now just plug in to your computer. Preferable in your home office not the office and work!

Back to the profile, what do you want a with man? You sit and think about this. Finally decide it's because there are times when you are lonely, it's easier to get some loving and attention, just someone to say goodnight to, if you are 'with' a man. You enjoy sex and don't want this part of yourself to be finished. It would be great to have a travelling partner and events would be more fun with someone to help carry the chairs and drinks. You find it difficult to cook for one and you would get more dinner party invites if you were not a single woman. 'Come on ladies, you hardly like your husband yourself so why, oh why, do you think I would want him'.

So, you continue the profile. Yes, you want a man, but you realise a lot of these needs could be filled by a woman too. So, what about a woman. Never really considered that. Hmmm that didn't take long and its considered, I like the manly parts a little too much, idea rejected, so here I am 'female seeking male'.

Now where was I? Body type. Fat. Floppy. Wrinkly. You choose curvaceous but that makes it sound like you think you're a sex goddess, so you go back to a bit overweight. He can work out which bit when you meet and he's off balance with your wit and charm and beautiful smile.

A smile is a big thing. How many first messages I get that say. 'I love your smile'. As a rule, most of the men have shocking photos of themselves. I once thought I was meeting a bald man but turned out he had a full head of hair. This was not noticeable because he took the photo under his chin and this viewpoint obliterated all signs of hair. He had balanced his phone on the steering wheel of his car.

I had just come out of lock down at the time and a certain amount of, 'I'm not doing that alone again,' gave him an in that he may not have got otherwise. Despite him having a good head of hair when I was expecting a bald head, he turned out to present as a lovely man and much better looking than I thought. His profile picture was terrible it turned out and one of the very rare occasions when he was much more handsome than his profile suggested. We dated a long time by the standard 'met online' date and when he eventually showed his true colours, I had sent him a few great pictures of himself. Of course, I was in these photographs, but I was gone from the scene when I saw that he had used them on his profile pictures a few weeks later. This relationship is another story for another chapter.

Sixty Single and Still Sizzling

Usually none of the men in the pictures are wearing a smile. What does this mean. Are they mean old bastards just looking for someone to screw and to cook for them, and not necessarily in this order either. Are they trying to look masculine and tough? Do they have any teeth? If they do are they false? Can I kiss a man with false teeth? Can I kiss a man with no teeth. This pattern of thought leads me to thinking about the art of kissing. I like kissing. Kissing is good, the forerunner to much more intimate pleasure. I do hate to be slobbered on, using your tongue is great and a passionate part of a great kiss but please, please don't lead with the tongue. Don't poke your tongue down my throat like it's a probe and you are seeking middle earth. Shit! Now I am thinking I must kiss these guys, so I start looking at their mouths with more interest. Smile damn you. Smile!

So, it Begins.

Trying to Sort the Good, The Bad and the Ugly and the Scammers.

UHOH Messages! 'Bigheart' has sent you a message. '69er' winked at you. Note here if someone has the name 69er on a dating site you are not interested. Fred introduced himself, 'Hi I am an oldie but a goodie' and Johnie43 has sent a 'flirt'. And now 69er, weirdo, has sent the first of many messages saying, 'I bet you'd be good in bed.' I did learn how to block people like him eventually but at first you know little about all this stuff. Blocking is an important skill. If you can't work this function out at first, google how to block someone on such and such dating site. There is lots of advice on doing this.

You are excited now, this is going to be so easy, you'll just read the messages, pick the one you want and with your wit and charm, that will be so evident even in the written word, that soon you'll be sitting back with the love of your life beside you, drinking cocoa and watching the Hobbit Movies, cos you both love them. Ah, you can see it already. Big mistake. You are now in the tricky part. You need to be calm attentive and careful.

Now you are emailing with Lennard, winking at Peter and fending off overseas messages that are mostly scammers and dreamers or men who just want to talk to you to eventually get you to talk about sex, then have long distance sex with them. Have you ever tried this? Relatively very unsatisfying when compared to the real thing but with a partner you are separated from for some reason it can be exciting and funny, certainly not something to be dismissed without consideration.

I was becoming quietly panicked by all this attention and I was given good advice by a lovely man who said, 'remember this, you don't owe anyone anything.' Trust your own instincts they are the ones to listen to and be on your guard always.

At first you try to answer all the messages, wink, flirts but it's too much and most of it is just nonsense. Eventually you stop opening every message and simply ignore winking and flirting. If the site is a paid site, then some of the winkers and flirters are not paid members. They need you to start a conversation with them. They want you to initiate the conversation so that they can respond. It is my opinion these individuals are cheapskates and should be ignored.

So, we will start with Lennard, i.e., 'Bigheart' you have talked with him on the onsite inbox and graduated to emails and after setting a meeting date exchange your mobile numbers. He seems nice, genuine. You write witty but relatively inane emails for a couple of weeks' because he lives in Perth, and this is a fair distance from you, and you don't want him to know too much about you until you meet him, your careful not to lead him on because that is so easily done. Meanwhile '69er' keeps sending random messages that say 'I bet you be good in bed' until you find out it is possible to block people like him. People that are stupid and incoherent and are just using your picture to get themselves off. A risk you take.

Another good reason for not leading Lennard on is that you are simultaneously talking to a very handsome, spunky engineer that life has dealt some very awful stuff up to.

Scammers

How to Recognise One or One Hundred.

He is a good-looking, muscles in all the right places, man who is some fifteen years younger than you. He lives in Sydney. Too far, you know, but he reassures you he will move heaven and earth to be with his true love if you just happen to be her. You begin to wonder why he has not been able to sweep a local girl off her feet and into his well-muscled arms and why he is messaging you, a beautiful woman for sure, but one in her 60's! You know that the likely hood of this being a legitimate match or even a real person are unrealistic, but you are already fantasizing about his muscles. He has a picture of himself drying off by the pool. Gorgeous!

Finally, you are ready to face the reality as he is now writing very long, detailed and well set out emails. No man alive ever writes more than a few lines and is always keen to get to the 'talking on the phone' stage because typing is not their natural means of communication. He mentions your beautiful smile and he loves your profile. The arty type suits him fine. He is into art. Well, you do have a beautiful smile and the photos you took at just the perfect angle do make you look pretty good so why not, you think. But the alarm bells are insistent and eventually they pierce the sexual frustration driven, deafness in your ears and you take a closer look at Mr Perfect.

Sixty Single and Still Sizzling

You become a detective. It's fun. You look up his name on google and low and behold you find a Facebook page that leads you to a website for his business which does look legit. But those long emails and now there are a few little errors, like what cancer his wife died from. In his first, long and well written email, it was Vaginal Cancer. You are not sure what this is, so you look it up. That's why you remember what it was originally. Now for a scammer this is a good choice because we are not really going to want to talk too much about this are we. In another email it is uterus. Hmm close together but not something you would mix up. Maybe it's a slip of the mind. Maybe he is genuine.

But you know he's not. So, you continue digging. Strangely though you can't access the website except via the FB page. This is not the usual way. He had in the beginning called you but quickly went to email. I asked my son to call the number and he was answered by what sounded like, an old person who did not speak good English. You know it's over. But those muscles! You check the ABN and the Affiliations and sure enough they do not exist or are in a foreign country and not pertinent to Australia. By now your, 'very close to the chest,' answers and your pointed questions have made him, it, her, realise the 'game is up,' but out of curiosity you check out the photos and read the names on the earth moving equipment and find that this is actually a genuine company. You call the company's receptionist. She acts a bit too surprised to find a scammer has used their images and job schedule. She asks, 'how did you know?' You tell her and she asks the name of the person who, in your imagination, is supposed to be a hunk just waiting to move interstate to have his way with you. When you say the name, she hangs up in your ear.

No one appears to care and most definitely not anyone on the dating site. But he did disappear from the site, and you are a whole lot smarter for the time you spent on this delightful person. I'm sure he reappeared a few days later with a new story, and a new picture. This rebirthing happens over and over. Some scammers use the same profile pic with a different name on the same site. A scammer is not always smart so watch for these alerts.

Lists and More Lists.

The Rules of Engagement
So, what do you do, you create a list.

Here is my first list. Your list may be different but once decided on try to stick to it. I did give in and break my own rules on meeting times now and then but mostly because of distance.

Always remember who you are. Trust your instincts. Remember you don't owe anyone anything. Tell the truth. (except about your age, I did not tell the truth about this, just a few years off but keep it sensible, remember the point of the exercise is to find Mr Right)

1. Talk only to people in your own State and preferable in the same area as you.
2. Only talk very general stuff and exchange first names and emails.
3. Only give your mobile number out when a meeting has been established.
4. Don't converse with anyone who can't meet you in the allotted time, and this no more than two weeks and you allow this amount of time only if distance and work commitments is part of the equation. Try to meet anyone of interest to you as soon as possible.

5. Don't video chat. The reason for not video chatting is because we do not look our best on these videos, neither does he. But there is a lot of other info to be gained from seeing inside a person's home, the clothes, furnishings, building type, area etc., Until you are ready to allow this person into your personal life and therefore space, keep him out of it.
6. Don't exchange pictures you don't want your grandkids to see.

I must tell you here that I have received some unsolicited pictures and the old saying, 'if you've seen one you've seen them all' is not true when it comes to men, and, or penises. You would think that the men are proud of their parts when they send them, but most are sadly disappointing, and they get the sender blocked without a backward glance. Some do get a second glance because you need a second look to check if what you are looking at is actually a penis, or a dead squirrel. True story. So here I will remind men to try to remember that women are not as attracted to the visual as men are when it comes to sexual imagery. I'm not speaking for everyone but for a large number of women this is true. You may think your personal parts are memorable but do some web searches and check out a few pictures for comparison.

More Lists

This time on Detecting Scammers.

Don't think the episode with the scammer from Sydney (or somewhere in the world) was a waste of time as it wasn't. All the detecting work I did has helped me to learn these things:

1. Do not give any money to anyone, nor access to any money or valuables.
2. You can upload any photo and find out where else it is on the internet, if it is on there, by using a simple google search. (You may find out that you are talking the person you are conversing with has used the image of the King of Persia. True story.)
3. There is a lot of information on the internet to help you, be scammer savvy.
4. No one seems to really cares about dating site scammers, and the sites administrators do not appear to care at all. This is my opinion and experience.
5. Scammers or crazy stalkers can build a new profile and be back online immediately with a different name.
6. It is easy to check ABN's and company registrations,
7. Affiliations can be checked out easily.
8. Trust your gut. Many of us have been mothers or fathers. We know when someone is not telling the truth.

9. If he looks too good to be true, he probably is, and the picture is most likely a fake and he could be a little old lady sitting with a team of scammers in a room full of computers.

Sadly, most young men, or indeed most sixty-year-old men, do not truly want to date a sixty-four-year-old, no matter what you look like or how fit and healthy you are. So please don't be the one who feels you are the exception to this rule. Older males have this same delusion, and young women (or a scammer) treat them the same way. On both sides of the coin, they are only interested in money. This is where commonsense ought to come into play. I always talked to my adult kids if I was not comfortable, and they were very helpful. If you don't or can't do this then have a good friend that you can run stuff by. Preferably an old friend that will tell you what you need to hear. Not what you want to hear.

I received an email from one person who I had initially engaged with, and he told me he was working on a skyrise building in a country town in my State. Interesting if you happen to know this town and its size and its likelihood of having a skyrise building. You could find someone who is working at a mechanical workshop on some remote island which you know isn't populated. One scammer sent me a lovely email asking me if I would consider helping my partner if they were in financial trouble. This type of scamming is too easy to pick. These are not the ones to worry about.

The scary ones are those who you date for a few weeks then, when you are finally relaxed and feeling secure in their company, they say things like, 'I'm short on my rent payment, can you help me for a few days?' This question or something like it, is usually plonked on you when you are least prepared for it. Usually after having had a lovely time together and you are completely off guard. You may be lying in bed together after a delicious lovemaking session and he says, 'Can

Sixty Single and Still Sizzling

I ask you something?' You are so off guard and the timing perfectly planned by him. You are in a vulnerable position, and this is what he or she wants. There will always be a great reason for this shortfall of funds, and he will be very embarrassed to ask you for help. My advice to is say, 'I have to think about that,' or straight out, 'No! I can't.' Be prepared in advance with a straight answer. If you do agree to give them money, then in most cases you will not see it or him again. Unless of course he feels that it was very easy to get this money from you and that you will most likely give him more.

There are a variety of good reasons, and not just losing the money, to consider a situation like this as not one you want to be in. Remember at our time of life we need to be able to look after ourselves in our old age. We cannot be dating a man that cannot even pay his rent. I am not saying we need to find someone who can provide for us, but we can't afford to find someone who we will have to support either.

I do feel strongly that being on relatively equal financial basis is a good start. This can be from the place where you both are very wealthy to where you both live on your seniors' pensions. It's about where each person stands in the relationship, naturally you want to stand together. Of course, if this is not your situation and you still feel that you both want to go ahead with a relationship then talk all of this out. Decide who, where and when. I had a friend who dearly wanted to travel with his new partner, he had the money, but she didn't. He wanted to pay for her so they could go together. She was not comfortable and didn't want to be indebted to him. As a couple perhaps that should not be the case and she could have accepted his kindness which also was to his benefit as he was sick of travelling alone.

First Meet Up.

When All the Work Comes to Fruition.

So, on with my story. While you are channelling these super detective skills you are simultaneously talking to the sweet man by email, remember Lennard? You have arranged to meet up for the first time. You are already travelling up to the city visiting family in Joondalup so this is where the coffee date will happen. He is happy to catch the train from South of the River. No matter how much you feel the person, male or female, you are catching up is genuine, the first date should always be in public.

The day has arrived, and your first dating experience is about to take place. You are so happy; you've finally got there, you've done it. You are going on a date. You're nervous. You look lovely. Your hair is perfect – glossy. You've just redone your eyebrow wax; your upper lip and chin is also waxed to perfection. Your fingernails and toenails are polished. You have just the perfect amount of makeup and you smell delicious.

You see him coming and your heart sinks, you know in that instance that it's not going to be a happy ending. You hope he has made the same decision. Because you are kind and because you need to have a cup of tea to get through saying 'there is no buzz' you sit down and smile. He's a nice man but you need that physical connection. You chat together and you learn he has an eight-year-old child. I simple do not do children under twenty-five, unless they are my adorable, do nothing wrong, blood of my blood, grandchildren, so you are happy there was no connection.

Conversation flows along quite easily which is a blessing and you realise he is a kind man, so you reassess, is there a way to make this work? But no, it's not going to work and as he tells you he has an appointment at the dental hospital as dentists are too expensive, you are glad of the first decision. He has a home and so I can't see how he can't afford one, six monthly, trip to the dentist, but he can't, so I wonder why. So unfortunately, the inability to take care of himself health wise, and a small child that he shares custody of to care for, coupled with no initial spark, you realise there are too many negatives. He is not the 'one'.

You discuss your feelings about the two of you as a couple, about connections and tell him you do not feel like you will be a match. He is a little put out by this and suggests feelings are overrated and at our age we should settle for compatibility. This is not what he should have said as I find this very frustrating and upsetting. It is annoying when people assume that, as you are over sixty, your emotional needs are no longer valid. There is that assumption that you can't fall in love. That at this age you must be practical. I am also really put off when people say, 'oh yes you just need a companion at your age'. I also need sex at my age. Sometimes I tell them that I do want a sexual partner and that I am as active now as I was in my forties, and they look shocked. This comes from women my own age. They act like their sexual parts have shrivelled up and died a long time ago. Well, theirs may have but mine are up and running, out and about and in need of attention. 'Settling,' is not an option for me. If I am not true to myself then who will I be true to and how and where is the start and end to settling. I am happy as I am, my life is great. I have no actual need for a man. I am not simply looking for sex, as this is easy to find, but I desire the whole well-rounded package, Mr Right. Just because I would love to have Mr Right in my life doesn't mean he can be any man. He must be the right one for me.

Ground Rules for Dating.

Make some Decisions Before you are Forced to.
You should always try to play on your home ground.

You must always keep your own moral standings whatever they may be. This is for your own benefit. Please know I have no judgement on anyone's actions. What you do is your business and the person or persons, you are doing it with. What feels good and comfortable for one maybe be abhorrent for another and vice versa. Just be sure of what you want, what you are agreeing to.

Let someone know where and when you are meeting a new person. Give them all the info you have on that person. And remember the first list. Meet in a public place.

Communicate. It is best to communicate early in conversation where you are at regarding engagement. I am talking here about engagement of the sexual kind.

I had a male friend tell me he dated a lady for some weeks, and they kissed and hugged and perhaps went to, 'third base,' (do you remember this from your teen years) they were quite intimate but, when he assumed they were about to go further and a 'home run,' was on the schedule, she told him that as, 'a Christian woman,' she was still married in the eyes of God, she couldn't, 'go all the way.' It would have been sensible, and respectful of her, to have told him this straight up and not lead him on. She thought as he was older, he would be happy with a mostly platonic relationship. He was not happy with this and from their interactions over the first few weeks she should have realised. She should have communicated. He was mad and it didn't end on a friendly note.

I have no issue with the idea of meeting up with someone whom, you have already decided with him or her, either via conversation, or indication, that is to be a purely sexual encounter. It may be a one-night stand or a long term 'friends with benefits arrangements, until you do meet Mr right. Sex is a delightful experience. One that does you good in all sorts of ways, both mentally and physically. Not to be done without. During my online experiences, I had two of the loveliest men as lovers. Not at the same time. Our arrangement was always, that if one of us decided we would become involved intimately with someone else, someone we thought maybe the one, our relationship stopped. Sometimes the relationship started again when, yet another prospective man bit the dust.

Remember in these wonderful experiences all the rules we established at the beginning of the search for love still apply. Your rules. Of course, you must agree together but don't give ground, or anything else, unless it is reasonable, and it works for you. For me it was wonderful to be sexually satiated. It was very helpful when meeting a new man as I was then able to look at the whole person without the sexual hormones wanting to jump in and cloud my judgement. Sex is only one part of a good partnership, an important part there is no doubt, but there are a lot more things that will need to be apparent as well. Sometimes when you are sexually frustrated you miss some of the obvious alarm bells.

As I said before all the names in this chapter both male and female are changed. You will not be able to recognise any of them, but you will relate to a lot of them. All the events happened but may not be recorded as having taken place with the same person

Sixty Single and Still Sizzling

as they did happen with or in the same situation in an attempt for ambiguity.

I won't beat around the bush here, the dating, the meeting up, is a bit of a nightmare, a game you must play and for me there were no ground rules. I had to wing everything, so I decided to play by my own rules.

When you begin the search for the elusive Mr Right, you do not realise that there are often more than two players in your new relationship. There are children, parents, yes some are still alive, stepchildren and other in-laws, who see you as a potential threat to them and their inheritance. There are friends of children who decide, or maybe are coaxed by other interested parties, it is their right to drop in unannounced and interrogate you. I have been investigated, abused, shouted at, told I was a liar, all sorts of stuff to which I never imagined I would be subjected. Most I took with a grain of salt and have forgotten about. One vicious, verbal attack by an invested, sister-in-law stands out as perhaps the most weird and random. She had already decided who he should be with. I was upset at the time but glad I saw the family for what it was. So be prepared, you never know who has a big sign saying, 'he's mine', on their head. In all these attacks I have never been confronted by another woman who thought the man was theirs, just family wanting their money intact. In some unusual cases family has decided, who with and at what time someone should re-enter the dating game, you come along and mess up their plans.

Now you are dating remember you have very little to go on as to who is who and who is safe and who is not. You have your own instincts and your common sense to look after you. Of course, there are family and friends that you can and should talk about who you are catching up with. I always informed my daughter of who when and where. Safety cannot be downplayed. If your children are as crazy as mine don't be surprised to look over your shoulder and see one or the other having a lunchtime coffee with friends three feet from you and your supposedly anonymous date. On one of my dates, I received a text message from my daughter with an image attached. This was an image of me having lunch with my friend. 'I'm in the next room.' she wrote. 'Oh, good one'. I replied.

Meetings for me were usually 'a coffee,' this is great because it is inexpensive, in the day light and can last as long or as short as you deem fit. You begin planning meetings with the focus and precision of a CEO's assistant. If you are good at it and plan well, you can have three catch ups in one day. One by one the prospects come and go, big ones, tall ones, fat ones, skinny ones, some resemble their picture, most don't, some you can't recognise. Most are older and have gained weight since, 'that one was taken at my son's wedding in 2004'. Almost none are an accurate depiction of the person you saw online. You begin to think this was the worst idea you ever had, and only crazy and desperate people are on the sites, but you think, 'I'm on it'. Am I desperate, you decide, I must be a little? After a while you sort of start to enjoy the meetings and life is fun and you decide to keep notes because an adventure this crazy must be recorded.

My second date of any significance and lasting longer than a coffee was with a man who decided he would like to drive down to my home to meet up with me. It's a lot of kilometres and I hoped for his sake we would hit it off. We have coffee and because he has come so far, lunch. All was going well. He was a huge man with several health issues which caused me some worry. I was trying not to be too hasty to decide he was not going any further than this initial date. While we were sitting and talking (he was talking a hundred miles an hour and only drew breathe occasionally to sip his tea) I realised that these health issues were backed up by several mental issues as well. Depression is the main one here. Your alarm bells are ringing loudly but your manners keep you making tea and smiling. As I love

Sixty Single and Still Sizzling

to write I also loved a good, interesting story and he had a very upsetting but unfortunately, common enough, story. I felt I did not need to know all of this on our first meeting, but he couldn't stop talking. He wanted to be honest which is great. He had been a victim of childhood sexual abuse at the hand of several religious sectors and the children's services, a sad story but he was fighting back, and I did feel empathy with him and his situation. Empathy is great but it is not the building block of a relationship other than friendship, and after lunch we, but mostly I, decided that this is where we would leave this one.

You continue to arrange meetings and as these go on you are amazed at the variety of men and their attributes, their audacity, and their ability to lie to your face. There are those that won't drive two kilometres unless 'there is something in it for them.' When you press for an answer to what it is they might want, and they won't answer the question you can surmise that it's is quick nookie and then bye-bye from them. There are the ones that talk to you for a while on the phone and then decide that there is no point in meeting you as you won't like them anyway as they, in their own opinion, are not that great a catch. As they have this opinion of themselves you are forced to agree with their own conclusion. What they are really saying is you are not for them.

I had arranged to meet a prospective 'love of my life' at my place of work, as I was closing for the day, and we could walk to a close by café together for coffee. We were going to go for a coffee as planned when he says, 'I don't drink coffee or tea let's just sit here'. I was not comfortable as it broke most of my rules but as it was broad daylight and the big windows opened to a busy sidewalk, I decided I would be safe. We sat at different ends of the couch. When he first arrived, he attempted to kiss me in a rather too friendly manner, so I said, 'just stop for a minute I'm not doing this at this point of our meeting.' We should wait and see what happens after we have properly met and talked'. He huffed at that and said, 'Why what's wrong with kissing?' When we did sit down, he remained at his end of the couch.

During our conversation which was all about him and his farm and how you could see the ocean, he sat at the end of the couch doing what appeared to me to be some sort of pelvic thrust. Just what you need when you are on your own with a strange man. I said, 'why are you doing that?' his reply, 'I have a sore back' I thought okay, how do I end this situation and get him out without having to make a scene. As if by magic our shop security cameras began to whirr and change positions. This made him jump up and look around. 'It's just the cameras.' I told him. 'As we are closed, they will be being monitored off site'. Of course, they weren't being monitored they were programmed to change direction at certain times during the day. It reminded customers that they were there. He became a little uncomfortable after that and said he had to go; work needed doing on the farm. Thank goodness for that. A few days later when thinking through the day and my date I realised that some of my members of my staff could get into the cameras via their mobile phones, and now and then they did. I must remember this in the future.

Just a side note here I know that we women can be like the men described and we end up with the same problems. There are a lot of people on the feminine side that are just not nice. I have made some great male friends and have listened to their stories. Their stories are included here and there in this book.

The Elephant in the Room

When it is the Right Time to Have Sex

One of my favourite men was a man around sixty-five, he had an awesome twinkle in his eye. He was thin and wiry; I like my men that way. I liked him immediately and after a few more 'coffee' dates that led to dinner dates we were ready to look at the idea of being intimate. This is a big step for me as I hadn't had sex with an actual person for a few years and to top it off he was to be the first 'cab off the rank' after my pelvic floor rebuild. This was not done as a cosmetic surgery but as a medical necessity. A pelvic floor restructure is not a simple operation and recovery takes time. He would be the first to see if everything was still there and indeed if it would all still work. Female friends who had undergone this surgery told me it was not always possible to just go back to 'how it was,' and sexual intercourse could be painful. Parts of your body get a little relocated as the tucks and tacks take place. Your clitoris can be shortened or lengthened as the muscles and various parts surrounding your vagina are manipulated to achieve the necessary result of the rebuild. Your sexual experience may not be the same or as good. It could be better but what are the chances of that, hey girls.

I knew it would be prudent to discuss this with him before we got into the bedroom as it would be a bit scary for him if I started yelling and screaming at the important moment. I began this difficult conversation asking him if I could discuss something important. I said, 'there is an 'Elephant in the Room,' situation and he laughingly said, 'yes, sure, why don't you address this situation.' He knew it was sex. I told him about the rebuild and that things may go haywire but reassured him that I knew there were more ways than one to skin a cat. I would not leave him hanging. So, to speak. He was sweet and reassured me that he would be careful and take my lead.

I went into the bedroom to undress, and he walked in with nothing on but his hat. He had a very big erection and I wondered how such a small man was still standing, there were no doubts about his readiness to indulge in some afternoon delight. I thought, 'help!' and dived for the bed and pulled the covers up over my head.

The sex was good, possibly because I was as a horny as hell. Getting used to a new sex partner is not always easy. Sometimes it works out sometimes it doesn't. He was not a fan of foreplay and later in our relationship when I mentioned that maybe a little more time spent on foreplay would be useful, he told me most women enjoyed his lovemaking techniques and were very satisfied with his expertise in the area.

During the time we were manipulating the sexual minefield of compatibility we continued to date. We got on great for a few months and I felt he may be the one. A big problem was that he was not interested in being part of my family. I am very committed to my family, my children and grandchildren and to a much larger family tree. I spent a lot of time at family events, and he would decline all invitations to these. He just wanted me, but I come as part of a great big, delightful package and I needed him to be a part of that as well.

He became jealous of my time and wanted me to be with him every moment. I broke up with him as I got sick of answering his questions as to where I was at any given time. He would text me and say, 'who are you fucking?' I owned my own business, and it was in hospitality, in the middle of tourist season. I barely had enough time to 'fuck' him. It was sort of encouraging that he thought I might have that energy. Eventually I couldn't be bothered justifying myself every two minutes, so I weighed the pros and cons, and decided it was all too hard. We broke up. It was sad as I really liked him and had put time and effort into our relationship. I knew he wouldn't be able to change, and I was not going to, so it was the right decision. He was angry and would not talk to me for a long time but eventually he understood and accepted his part in the breakup. This did not leave me unscathed, and I was upset for a long time. We do still talk occasionally. Just recently he has informed me that he has a pair of my knickers that I left behind one weekend. He says, 'I washed them.' I'm glad of that I answer.' 'Can I collect them? 'No, I like them'. I asked him if he liked to wear them and as our conversation continued, he told me they were souvenirs, he had a drawer full, all neatly folded, washed and ironed. Only one pair were mine. Could be creepy and yes maybe it is. But there is no harm in it and if we ladies can leave without our underwear what do we have to say.

Oh, just a heads up, men love to talk at length about their sexual conquests, but you mustn't ever do that. Mentioning former lovers and how they did this and that is a definite no for you. You're a woman. Sexual freedom is not for you. Remember women of our era barely have a vagina let alone a clitoris or an orgasm. I've added this here because one of the arguments he used against me when we broke up was that I talked too much about men. I now and then did share a particular funny or exciting incident with him, in relation to my sexual encounters but this was always on the back of one of his stories on the same subject.

Later when discussing this with different male friend he told me that discussing openly about previous lovers was a thing I should never do. So, despite the fact, that, at sixty with three children and two marriages, according to the man I'm making love to at any particular time, he's the first. He is also, and most definitely, the best I ever had. And sometimes it is good to tell him so.

More Meet Ups

And More Dead Ends.

So now the endless meetings restart. During this period where I was not seeing anyone, I met Teddy, he was a straight down the line type of guy with an opening message that you either responded to or not. He wrote, 'Hi I am looking for a woman who likes sex and is up for a no commitment relationship.' A friend with benefits sort of deal. I was not seeing anyone so responded with, 'Yes, I'm interested but on condition that I'm still looking for Mr Right, and when I meet him, we stop'. If somehow miraculously the 'one' appears, we are off, its closed doors then, no connection, no fuss and no falling in love along the way'. I was around 10 years older than him and he in his mid-50's still had the dream of a happy family with little Teddies running around. I must admit he was a sweet man in all the ways you can be, and I did fall just a little bit in love.

We lived in different towns which was great, small towns have big eyes and ears, so we decided to meet in the middle.

I had little experience up to this stage of my life, let's be truthful here, I had no experience with this type of rendezvous. I told my eldest daughter where I was going and that I was meeting up with a man, as I went on lots of dates, she didn't ask many questions. I think it's wise to tell someone where and what you are doing and to check in on arrival and throughout the time for safety. Send through a picture and any info you have like car rego etc., let the person know you have done this. Male or female you should do this.

We met at a motel; he had checked in already, so I went directly to the room. On my way I received a few texts saying stuff like, 'shit are we actually doing this?' You are coming, aren't you? Should I be naked when you get here? I am naked now!' All of these made me realise we were both on uncommon ground.

I arrived and said very little, just undressed and kissed him, we then took a shower together and as the saying goes, 'the rest is history.' Teddy and I were lovers on and off for about two years. The off parts were when one of us wanted to explore the possibility of having found the man, or in his case the woman, of our dreams. I will be truthful here and tell you my morals were better than his as he would often ask why we had to stop. Part of the reason was my moral conscious coming onto play. Then the logistics of two relationships, I had limited down time as it was and felt if you don't give something your best attention then you can't complain when it goes belly up. I was also in my sixties so did not have the same needs as I did when I was thirty. There is also the issue of safe sex and who and where you need a condom. Bad to get mixed up.

Take note here if you are planning to use a condom you will usually have to take care of this side of things yourself. Most men, older ones especially, think that they don't need a condom, sort of like, if you only have sex once every now and then you are safe. They also assume that the woman they slept with last month only had sex with them anyway, so she was safe, and moreover, they hate condoms. I am not a lover of them either, but to not use one you must trust the man or woman you are intimate with to be honest with their sex lives and encounters. It is important to understand that you are having sex with every person who your lover has had sex with and so on for the last six months at least. Could be no one else but it could be thousands of others.

Sixty Single and Still Sizzling

The 'on' part of my and Teddy's hooking up, our friends with benefits, situation, was when we were not seeing anyone else. I still get a text occasionally asking if all is well. He is in a relationship now and appears happy. He once messaged and said he missed me and the things we did and how we felt together, he said he wished his new partner was like me, I suggested he ask her for what he wanted but it seemed he was afraid to do this. I told him I was willing to call her and give her some hints. Unsurprisingly he wasn't up for that either, but it was fun to tease him a little.

So, despite having Teddy to keep me satisfied I continued to seek out that elusive, desirable, unlikely to exist, Mr Right. And no, Mr Right did not have to be Mr Perfect but had to be perfect for me.

During this time, I met Alan. Alan had driven about five hundred kilometres to see me and take me to lunch which he organised at the most exclusive and expensive restaurant we had in our town. He was a lovely, big man, kind-hearted and genuine. While having lunch with Alan I misplaced my foot on what I thought was a step but was a hedge plant between the steps. I fell backwards and was flat on my back at his feet. Even to this day he loves to tell people, 'I had her on her back on the first date'. Alan and I did not get together as partners, but we have over a few years become good friends. We catch up every few months for a life events exchange and enjoy each other's company. He has a lovely partner now. It has taken her a while to accept our relationship as friendship, but she is cool with it now. Now that I am in a full time, committed, we've bought a home together, committed, relationship.

During our time as good friends Alan and I travelled to Bali together and we had a great time. It was not a sexual encounter; we enjoyed each other's company. We had the pleasure of someone to go to dinner with or have a swim with, to go exploring with and to share costs. I found most of my friends found it difficult to understand how we could do all this together yet not have a sexual relationship. Alan was a great conversationalist, and a perfect gentleman, except for the time he tried to sell me to our driver who thought I was a great catch.

Alan and I exchange stories of our dating experiences. There is one that he experienced which I feel compelled to share. He met a lady online. She was the first to contact him, and after some initial chit chat back and forth they agreed to meet up for coffee.

He tells the story like this, 'I was sitting at the table waiting for this small, black, African lady to arrive. A shadow was cast over the room as a very large lady fills the doorway, blocking the light. Surely not, I think. But yes, she makes her way up to my table. She seemed a happy go lucky lady and certainly was not showing any hesitation to meet me face to face. I asked her when her picture was taken, she starts laughing happily and all sorts of things started jiggling away, she told me that it was about twenty-four years and about five stone ago, at her daughter's wedding. Oh, I said, did you think I wouldn't notice. She just laughed and said I wouldn't be here if I put myself on as I am now. Fair enough. So, as I am a big man myself and as I'm not about to hurt her feelings we had our coffee together. I was surprised by her lively personality, and I enjoyed talking with her. She was an immigrant and as such had little money and no pension yet, she was living with her daughter, and she was looking for a way out of this domestic situation by finding an Aussie man willing to take her in. Even though this made me a bit wary I felt another day out would be okay. We decided to go to the movies later that week.'

'I picked her up and we had just got engrossed in the movie, well I was the one engrossed in the movie, she was looking into moving her plan to find a man to keep her onto fast forward. Without so much of a heads up, my felt my trousers zipper being opened, and before I could react, her hand is inside my trousers grasping my penis. I nearly jumped off the chair and pulled her hand away from me, firmly

Sixty Single and Still Sizzling

rezipping my trousers and telling her that this is not the time or place. She said she thought I would like it. I was taken aback; I didn't really know how to react to what had happened. Let's just watch the movie, was all I could muster. I'm not a prude and like my sex as much as any man but two 65-year-old people in a relatively empty theatre in broad daylight getting and giving a hand job is not my style at all.'

When the movie was over, we went outside, and she confidently said, 'Okay, let's go to yours so we can finish what I started in there.' I said, 'You did not start anything. You have certainly finished something.' I'll drive you to your home and that's it.' She was quite angry and accused me of using her. I was moved to laughter with this statement. She had just sexually assaulted me, and I was the bad guy.'

Despite this unsettling encounter Alan continued with his quest for a lifetime friend and partner. He has found a lovely lady who suits his lifestyle and temperament. They travel around in a large motor home and life's good. He had a successful conclusion to a long search. He was on the site, on and off, for six years. I hope he never has to return.

Things You Do for Love.

But Mostly the Things you Won't Do for Anything

Chad was a weird man. He wanted a relationship, but he wanted no commitment. This is not possible, but soon one understood that he wanted a permanent woman in his life but also one that he was able to hold at arm's length from the family's fortune. Obviously, the sons wanted this as well, so no driving to his house for an unplanned visit. We didn't last long, a few dates and one very unsatisfactory night of him kissing me with his tongue darting around my mouth in short stabbing movements. Like a frog trapped in a tin. To this day have no idea what he thought he was doing.

I was on holidays for a few weeks in a seaside town, my single sister came down on the bus to visit and we talked about online dating and how it worked. I logged into my profile, changed my location and we did a search of all the available men in this region. We found a man in his late 60's that was looking to catch up with a lady for, what he had described as a long-term commitment. We chatted online then agreed to meet for lunch next day. We met down at the foreshore where there are a lot of people going to and fro. My sister

Sixty Single and Still Sizzling

came along, and I had told the gentleman that she was with me. He seemed unphased with that. If he was thinking two for the price of one, he never gave that feeling away during our lunch. He was a portly man, not unattractive, but not God's gift to us all, either.

We chatted away and he appeared to be an interesting character until I asked about his situation and what he was looking for in a relationship. He was keen on having a lady that would spend time with him in his apartment. Spend time, not 'live with.' His wife, yes still married as a divorce would split the family fortune, lived on the family farm and his son now ran the farm. I asked how comfortable his wife would be with him having a mistress and he said she would not need to know. So, here's the scene he has created. He wants a woman for sex and company, for this, the woman gets the same. No visits to the family farm or the daughter's wedding, just an in the background role with no future in it. No possibility of a love story here. Protecting the family fortune is more important than anything else. This may suit some of you, but I am not a girl to stay out of the limelight. I am, according to my first husband, 'a high maintenance woman'. With this gentleman I did appreciate his straightforward honesty about his situation.

Another man who I thought was a good prospect, a glimmer of a hope, a chance that he would be the one, ended up in the same disappointing pile as the others. He liked to play bridge and played in a lot of tournaments. This made him unavailable quite a lot and I thought if we were going to have a chance at any relationship, I would have to learn to play bridge. Unbelievably coincidental there was a bridge course for beginners in my town. I know! It's amazing how the universe works and, in this case, has a very sharp sense of humour. I thought it was a sign from above, or somewhere. I excitedly put my name down and was reassured that, even though I had missed the first class, I would catch up. I had to avail myself of a certain book and I could borrow one from the teacher while mine was coming in.

I went to collect the book that was left out, lovingly protected from wind and rain, by a plastic bag and a large brick on his doorstop. My first lesson came, and I was early to the group. Eager to begin my journey to world champion bridge player.

Have you ever played bridge. A more complicated game and more boring game cannot be found. I soon realised that it was better to not try to win so that you could win by allowing your opponents to try to win and therefore they would lose, and you would win without any risk. I also realised that you spent many games with your cards on the table while your so-called partner played alone. I also learned that laughing and sighing deeply or saying, 'For Fucks Sake,' were a no-no and that the teachers, students and players were extremely serious about the unwinnable, except by losing, game.

This did not have a happy ending. I never caught on to the game or a reason why people played it. I put my new copy of, 'How to Play Bridge' book on the library shelf. I also carefully rewrapped my loaner copy and returned it to its place under the brick on the doorstep of my bridge teacher. My new, bridge playing, friend never had enough time for me and without discussion we drifted away from each other.

A friend told me he met a woman who only wanted to have him around on Wednesdays and Fridays. She wanted her weekends to herself. Occasionally she would like him to accompany her somewhere on the weekends. I feel she needed a gigolo not a boyfriend. My friend agreed with this interpretation of the situation and the prospective partner got sent off to resume her search for a slave. There would be situations where this may work but it would have to be agreeable to both parties and at least in her case she communicated early in the relationship. No real harm done in this case.

I had coffee with a rather overweight man with heart disease and several other medical conditions due to his weight. I know all of this because as he hit the table he started talking and telling me his troubles. Health troubles and mental troubles, family troubles and trust issues. He went on and on. He was not selling himself perfectly and I wondered why we were here. Perhaps having looked at me he thought I have to put her off, I'm such a catch I must tell her all this stuff to get away before she flings herself on me.

Then without drawing breathe he says, 'I like you; you are very attractive I hope we do get together but if we do I have to tell you I have some issues in the sex department'. I say, 'stop this is not necessary at this stage,' but he won't stop. He goes on, 'Well I have to tell you I do like sex, and I can look after you in this department, but I have erectile dysfunction largely due to the medication I take for different things.' At these words I begin looking around the café, hoping no one else is listening and trying to find a rock to crawl under, willing him to stop, but it gets worse. 'Don't worry,' he says. 'I have a sexual counsellor and he says there is a needle you can inject me at just the right time so I will be able to fulfill your needs and my own of course.' I squirm, I am needle phobic at any time and putting one into a floppy penis while laying back moaning in pleasure from our intense lovemaking is an unimaginably hilarious thought. All I want to do is escape but he is smiling widely like a good boy who has told the truth and now, needle in hand, I'll reward him with a quick nookie out the back. I'm sure he still can't understand where he went wrong on that date. He is still floating along on the image of finally getting someone to give him that needle, just at the right moment. Just another day in the ridiculous world of online dating.

A male friend met a lady online and they talked on the phone a few times. They did not meet up as she lived a few hundred miles away in the city and he in the country. He did not give his address but used his own name. She somehow tracked him down and a few mornings later, without invitation or notice, she arrived at his home. Her car filled with her belongings.

He was a bit surprised but after a brief and angry discussion which ended with him telling her he was not interested in her as a partner at all now, especially when she was prepared to act in such an unsolicited and uninvited way. She certainly could not stay with him. She went into hysterics about being late at night and nowhere to go so he gave in and told her she could stay the night; she slept in the house, and he slept in his van. The next morning without too much preamble he sent her crying loudly down the driveway. He was an uncaring arsehole apparently.

One of my male friends wanted to move in with his partner, they had been together a couple of years, and he was getting tired of driving up and down about a one hundred and sixty kilometre round trip. He slept over often but still had to go back home. She did not want to move as having her own home gave her security she explained. I understand this. They came to an understanding when she finally told him that she did not want anyone else to know they were living together, and he purchased a small home in the same area. He then moved in with her. To keep it all in order he paid her a weekly rent, it was not a small rent and was meant to cover for food and added utilities. In truth it was to protect her from him having any claim at all on her property, when they parted if, and when, they did. He still had his own home to take care of. He also paid for all their outings, travel and meals This was a win, win for her and even though he could see this disparity he tried to make it work. He was reasonably well off and had genuine feelings for the woman. It did fall apart however as he wanted a more active retirement with lots of travel and she was a home body. He sold his home in the area and has moved on.

For me I think sometimes you have no choice but to take a risk. You can do all you can to protect yourself, but it may or may not work out that way. If you are in love and trust your new partner, you will not set up all these barriers.

Sixty Single and Still Sizzling

So on with the story. One of my partners had, what I thought was called a CRAP machine, you must laugh at this name, it is a perfect name for such a weird contraption. I am now sadly aware it is called a CPAP machine. Now I'm sure using this devise is better than dying but I would suggest that it is only just better. Sexual spontaneity is impossible with this machine in the room. This man also liked to get up in the night and eat cheese. I know!

Sometimes you meet a decent man, and you think okay can we work this all out. This happened with a man who we will call Jason. I liked him but I was not convinced we had enough in common to go the long haul. I was attracted to his artwork and the beautiful poems he wrote. On one of our early meetings at which we spent a fun afternoon together, talking and having a walk around town. In my heart I knew that we would not be a match as he was happy in his small town and in a quiet retirement. He had no desire to travel and me, I have got itchy feet. The world is full of amazing and interesting, beautiful, and terrifying things. I would love to experience as many as I can. Not so much the terrifying ones of course. I did not want to start a relationship I knew would be doomed to fail. He had assured me I was welcome to go traveling and do anything else I liked in the future, and he would be fine with that, but I would have to do it alone. I already did that, and I was not a loner type of girl. This, doing everything by myself, was one of the reasons I was seeking a partner.

During the first week when I was trying to see if there was a way forward and I was making up my mind on him, he drew an attractive if not totally accurate picture of me. I liked it and said so. I already knew, from my previous relationships that you cannot change anyone so I was trying to find a way I would be satisfied with the sedentary, staying at home, enjoying pottering in the garden, lifestyle. I decided finally, we would not work out as a couple as it would not be enough for me. I was already visualising a long trip around Australia. After I told him this, he redrew the picture of me via a computer program, I was ugly and distorted with a very scary set of double chins. At first, I thought, 'what a Dickhead,' and I was angry with him. I showed my daughter the pictures and she started laughing so hard that I too saw the funny side and had a good laugh. Laughing at yourself can be liberating. This was one of those moments.

Problems of a Different Kind.

Erectile Disfunction Raises its Head, (or not).
I've taken about 5 minutes to google information about erectile disfunction and premature ejaculation. The reason I'm telling you about the small amount of time I have taken is because I want to make a bit of a point. It does not take long to get some good information.

Now, I know that you can't believe everything you read on your PC but the evidence from many of my sources, including men I have spoken openly with, regarding this, confirms the information I found online.

Erectile dysfunction and premature ejaculation are common sexual dysfunctions that can affect men of all ages, but it happens way more often in older men. Erectile dysfunction affects the ability to achieve or maintain an erection that is firm enough for sexual intercourse, while premature ejaculation simply means ejaculation occurs sooner than desired during sex or even during foreplay or just thinking about sex. Both are undesirable and can be embarrassing.

Neither of these two conditions are inevitable for everyone, but they are considered a normal part of aging. Risks factors are conditions such as cardiovascular disease, diabetes, and the use of medications that treat high blood pressure, chronic pain, prostate disorders, and depression. Long term use of alcohol and tobacco and other drugs can contribute to these conditions. Being stressed, feeling anxious even being overweight can be a big factor.

It's important to communicate with your partner about your sexual health and any concerns you may have. It's also important to remember that the right female or male partner will not fix ED or PE. These conditions are medical issues and require professional treatment. Almost all the information I read pointed men toward their General Practitioner.

In addition to getting medical advice there are steps you can take yourself to improve your sexual health. _ It is entirely up to you to make the choices to have a healthier lifestyle by eating a balanced diet and getting regular exercise. Take up meditation or yoga or tai chi (my favourite) give up smoking if you still indulge and watch your alcohol consumption. The question for each to answer for themselves is, how important is a great sex life to me.

Remember that communication is key in any relationship. By talking openly with your partner about your sexual health concerns and working together to find solutions that work for both of you, it is possible to enjoy a fulfilling sex life at any age. Think back to my 'elephant in the room' situation, open, honest communication prior to hopping in bed, made this a fun experience.

When I had decided to write down my experiences and perhaps bring them together in a book, I began to ask more people more questions. I had a discussion with a man who was willing to tell me about his own problems, how he felt and how he found having to have these talks was an embarrassment. He said, 'you always hope things will go as planned. You hope that your body will respond to your mind.' He however agreed that this was rarely the case and that he would have felt less embarrassed if he had talked about his situation before they got into bed together instead of waiting until the point when nothing was happening, and he had to admit his condition.

As we continued to discuss the topic of mature sex he told me some stories of couples, some had been together for years, some newly together. One man had no problems strapping on a dildo to allow his wife to enjoy sex the way they had enjoyed for years. He told me he would do that if his partner desired him to when and if the time came along where it was necessary. I remember I recalled the story to a friend, who was a little horrified, he said, 'tell him you'll strap on a dildo and see if he likes that,' This made me laugh so much that I knew it was time to start to record notes, I realised that it was moments like this that make a great story. Another story this gentleman shared with me was of an older couple who, as the man was still sexually active and the female was not, would put aside a portion of their combined pension so that once per month he could go to his favourite brothel. This is wonderful. If both parties can work out a solution that works for them, who are we to judge.

As for me I had little to no experience with this condition until I began to date men in their later years. I have now had a little too much experience with ED and PE. ED and PE are not always together but occasional they can decide to get together just to make everything that little bit more complicated. I am not unsympathetic to these serious and debilitating problems for men. ED is a frustration where one feels arousal and sexual desire, but the penis doesn't come to the party. He just stays in bed won't even bother to see whose there. Or in the case of PE, he 'comes' along, doesn't really get involved but leaves his mess at the door. So, although I have some sympathy, I strenuously ask men to take control of this issue, they must research and talk to their doctors and specialists. In many cases the underlying issue is emotional or due to weight, medicine or simple lifestyle. It is not up to me to be counselling you at this point. Men must take responsibility for their own issues and if any of these conditions is going to be part of the sexual encounter, they ought to have some conversation with their intended partner before getting undressed.

I recall one incident which could have been seriously funny and could have led to huge dismay and embarrassment if I was not such an easy going and kind person. I had been dating a man I met online. He was over six feet tall and overweight. As the relationship led down the path to a sexual encounter, he was often reluctant to take things all the way to a sleep over. I must admit I did eventually push the issue; it was time. We were in or we were out. I was not wanting a purely platonic relationship at this point in my life and not now, especially after the six-week covid lock down, and who knew how much more of this was to come. We finally got to the part where we go that last step. I admit I was keener than he was. Maybe I'll rephrase this. He was keen but worried about his ability to hold it all together, so to speak. Eventually he got his courage up and we decided that we would have a sleepover on the weekend as I could have Sunday off.

One thing I have noticed with sex in my later years it is often a more planned event than a spontaneous one. It could be for work reasons, fatigue, older children around, all of this. I have thought this through, and I am not against this planned interaction, I must admit, however, that now and again it's nice to be swept off your feet and into the bedroom.

But back to this one interaction. I remember the day clearly. It is embedded in my brain forever. I wore a dress I particularly liked as it was long and floaty, and I looked good in it. The soft material and the style hid a lot of faults. After some initial kissing and cuddling over a glass or two of wine we decided to take it to the bedroom. Everything had been going along well until we got our clothes off. I was greeted by a very small penis. I wondered whether having sex was even possible. As I said he was a large man, so this exasperated the problem of the tiny appendage.

Now I am not a person to put anyone down or deliberately embarrass them, so I did not react to this disappointing and problematic sight. I did not wish to make him feel bad or inadequate so I carried on regardless but let me tell you I was really racking my brain as to how I would cope with this situation. I thought well maybe he'll do something surprising, and I won't mind the size. I liked him, and I did not want to do anything that may hurt or scar him for life. I decided to go with the flow. I must admit to a certain amount of curiosity as to where this, 'Flow,' would lead. How could we work through what I perceived to be problem. He, however, did not seem concerned and certainly never looked uncomfortable.

Murphy's law come into play here as Murphy said, 'if things can get worse, they will,' because things could get worse, and they very quickly did. We had barely undressed and laid back onto the pillows when he suddenly launches himself on top of me and he is ejaculating as he gets into position. For some inexplicable reasons he believes that this moment is the time to tell me that he suffers from premature ejaculation and erectile disfunction. I had figured all of this out in about the two seconds that he took to come and go. I was at this point disappointed and frustrated. I was in the mood for sex. He should have told me what to expect. He said he was embarrassed but this had not stopped him from going ahead with what he knew would not be a good ending, for me especially. This lack of respect for me, in combination with the small penis did not promise any great sessions in the bedroom or indeed a long relationship.

This one-sided attempt of lovemaking was an entirely disheartening experience. Any amount of conversation beforehand would have helped us both to handle the occasion better.

In an effort to help him I suggested he have a long chat with his doctor to see what, if anything, could help this rather untenable condition. After some reluctance on his part and many excuses like having to take time off work, it's hard to get an appointment, I'm sure it will sort itself, and such silly excuses he finally got the courage to go. The Dr prescribed Viagra. It did help somewhat.

We were getting along well in other areas so I wanted to see if the relationship could go further if we shared our issues and worked together. The problem here is he did not act honestly and was taking other medication that he had not talked about. This sort of overplayed the Viagra and all in all lovemaking was never satisfactory. We did try for a little while but there was rarely a happy ending for me. I decided that we should go our separate ways and continue the quest for the partner that met each of us perfectly. There were other issues as well but this one seemed insurmountable.

There are lots of loving ladies out there who want a platonic relationship. The problem with that idea is that most men think that their problems will all go away with the right partner. In their own opinion there is really nothing wrong with them anyway. I've often heard it quoted, 'It's natural to be a bit slow at my age.' They want their partner to be sexually active in the hope that this will be the answer to their situation.

Don't Judge a Book by its Cover.

Or by the First Few Chapters

I met Jonathon as few months after we came out of our first six weeks isolation period in 2020. Perhaps my determination not to spend any more weeks in isolation all by myself had clouded my judgement but I saw a happy and reasonably attractive man. When he got out of the car, I thought this is surely the wrong man as in his picture he appeared to be bald, but this man has a full head of white hair. He is sixty, which is a few years younger than me. He sort of 'rocked and rolled' towards me and I wonder what on earth do we have here.

    I worked out on further inspection of the photo that he has taken his profile pic from under his chin thus making him appear bald. His photography skills are sadly lacking as is common with men. They don't want to ask anyone they know to take a picture for them as they are not wanting anyone to know they are on a dating site. Wake up gentlemen, most of the country's population, male and female and all others, married, divorced or single, is on the online dating network.

    Johnathon was at least smiling in the picture. The jerking, rocking and rolling walk I later discovered, was the result of two hip surgeries and one knee reconstruction. I liked him, and we had a freely flowing easy conversation over lunch. Eventually we started dating and over a month or so we got to know each other.

As our relationship continued, I began to see we had sort of run out of things to talk about and I realised he was not well travelled, and that he had no ambition to improve on that situation. He had no ambition at all really. I should have seen the alarm signals, but I missed them. He was not well educated but this is not always the key to interesting and enthusiastic life. I had been told by some friends that, 'I had a type.' I was trying to not always date the same man in different clothing. Because of this I paid little attention to any of these differences.

While we were dating, he invited me to meet his daughter who was travelling to town. He was very nervous and making all sorts of comments, some not very nice, about how judgemental she was, how she was like her mother, who was a bitch (in his opinion). He was really stressed leading up to the dinner and this, had me on edge. Well, all I can say is it did not go well. She lived up to his description and he hardly spoke to her throughout the meal. When I tried to talk with her, she was rude and dismissive. Horrid night all round. I am telling you all of this because later when it all went to shit, he accused me of being rude to her. Later I met another of his daughters, and she was very kind. He was relaxed around her; I never did work all this out.

We continued our relationship for a few months; I was extremely busy with my business, so I just went along with things as they were, not perfect but not awful either. I was selling my business which was a full time and extremely stressful entity, and which involved me working in some way every day of the week. I felt we would have more time when I was free of it. Then when I had more free time, I thought I would be able to sit back and reassess our relationship and perhaps sort any small stuff out.

Sixty Single and Still Sizzling

We had a great time at a big Blues festival where, amongst the usual music festival activities, a miracle occurred two mornings in a row, four double yolker eggs were cracked while I was making breakfast in the Bed and Breakfast, I thought this was a sign of good things to come. I like going to this festival and I plan from year to year, you can't get any accommodation if you don't do this. I had bought our tickets and paid for the Bed and Breakfast. I did not mind this as I was always going to be going. We had fun, went out dancing, where he trod on me like he always did, and we laughed and enjoyed it all.

A few weeks after this and about six months into our relationship everything fell into a seriously deep hole. There was no way out of this chasm. All had seemed fine, but as my business became just too busy, I asked him to not come to my home on Friday night as he usually did. I told him I had a lot more work to do than usual and I would need to bring it home with me and on top of this I had some early meetings with a prospective buyer. This would mean an earlier start than usual the next morning. He insisted he wanted to come and see me, he would bring his own dinner and be very undemanding, he just wanted to be there. I agreed, how could I not. The whole time on the Friday night he was a bit of a nuisance and seemed unhappy with all sorts of things. I did not have time to take any notice at this point. On Saturday morning he snapped at me and when I asked him, 'What is going on with the crappy mood?' he angrily replied, 'My back hurts!' I said, 'Okay I'm sorry but don't snap at me for caring.' As I drove off to work, he was all 'lovey dovey' and kissing me as usual, saying things like, he can't bear to leave me, and the day would be a long one before I got down to his house. He was his usual loving, over the top, self. I went off to work leaving him to sort himself and go home. I was planning on going to his house to spend Saturday night and Sunday with him.

It is significant now that I was singing away to Queen's, 'Another One Bites the Dust,' as I arrived at his place. I was happy looking forward to the night and time we would spend together tomorrow. As I came in, he was talking loudly to a friend on the phone. He greeted me with hand signals to be quiet. He was clearly agitated and not his usual self. I could see his was drinking scotch. Unusual for him to drink in the middle of the day. I sat down and when he finished his very long conversation, he sat in his chair with a sour, pouting face. Ignoring his attitude, I decided to act like all was well, which clearly it was not. I said, 'Don't I get a kiss or a hello then?' He dragged himself up with such reluctance I asked, 'are you injured?' 'No, I am tired.' Was his angry retort. Tired of me it turned out. He went into the kitchen with the bottle of Prosecco I had brought along and began to pour me a glass. He was clearly upset so I came into the kitchen beside him, he was putting ice in the drink, I said, 'no ice hon,' at which he scooped out the ice with his fingers and practically threw the glass of Prosecco at me. Paradoxically he was yelling at me that he knew not to put ice in the drink. I took the drink and went back to sit on the couch, there was nowhere else to sit as the house was small. I was expecting him to sit beside me and explain what he was upset about and say something like sorry this or that has happened and I'm a bit upset. Instead, he said very angrily, 'We need to talk!' 'Everything in my life is all about you.' 'Okay,' I calmly responded, 'Tell me what you mean by this. What have I done to upset you?' During my working life I have done a lot of courses regarding conflict management so slipped into my diplomatic self and tried to stay calm.

He began shouting at me and telling me I was a bitch, always undermining him and such. I tried to calm him and get some sense as to where and what I had done to bring on this outburst of fury, but he was working himself up into a rage, and I could see no end to it.

Sixty Single and Still Sizzling

Up until this point in some six months of seeing each other we never had an angry word.

I said, 'I'm going to go home now as you are clearly very upset with me, I'm not making anything better by being here.' Now this may seem heartless but a huge man attacking you, full on, crying and red in the face, snot and tears coming from all over, was scary. I was shocked, and I was afraid. I was feeling a rising fear and alongside this fear I was confused and becoming angry. I knew I had to get out before it was escalated into something else. I had never even imagined this side of Johnathon so who knew what there was to come. I grabbed my bag and was trying to get out the door, I got passed him because he was madly gathering anything that was mine to throw at me. At the same time, he was shouting, 'Just like that you're going to leave me?' Honestly, I had no idea what to do, he was incoherent by now and my stuff was landing in my bag and around me. I was running for my car. I jumped in and tried from the safety of the car to get him to calm down and take some breaths but he was not going to be talked down from this self-righteous rage.'

I sat in the car, trying to control my shaking hands and to get the car started. It was quite a new car and for a moment I forgot I didn't need the key in my hand to start it. That was good because I was shaking so much, I would not have been able to work it. Anyway, with him yelling and screaming after me I managed to start the car and I took off down the driveway and out of his gate and his life. I drove directly to my son's home and he and his partner consoled me with what I already knew, Johnathon was a bloody idiot. I drank a bottle of wine with them, slept on the couch and drove home the next day.

That morning I was going over the events in my head and I decided the personality change was inspired by a mix of Scotch and Viagra. Later I discovered that he was on an anti-depression medication. Maybe he had stopped the anti-depression pills that he had not thought to mention to me in all our time together. I found this out because at this point, I was really concerned for his safety, I messaged a good friend to go to his home to make sure he was okay. His friend said, 'great he's gone off the rails again.'

On Monday I received a text from Johnathon asking to talk and I agreed that we should, but at a public place, I would meet him at a local cafe at midday. He texted me back saying that he 'was too emotionally distressed to meet in public,' Could I come to his house. I replied by text. 'That's okay, we can meet another day, but I am not coming to your place to talk. I am happy to wait until you are feeling capable of talking in a place of my choice.' He never did get over his emotional distress.

He did however manage to maintain the rage long enough to try to tell me off over the phone. I was amazed at his stupidity as he rang early in the morning at precisely the time that he knew I would have arrived at my business to get sorted for the day. He began screaming at me down the phone. I said, 'I'm busy at work right now, can we please talk later in the day?' He ridiculously said that it was my fault and problem that I had to work today, not his, so I said, 'I'm going to hang up know.' I hung up, he rang back. I hung up, he rang back. Frustrated with this childish behaviour and being not at all comfortable with the situation I asked him, 'In what world do you think I'm going to hold the phone while you yell bad stuff at me.' I kept hanging up. I eventually had to block his number but there are a lot of places where you can contact someone these days, and it took a while to block all access.

In one of his hysterical shouting bouts that managed to get through before I hung up very quickly, he told me that his children and even his mother hated me. His mother is ninety-three, we have met only once. She invited us for lunch. Johnathon was excited for me to meet his mother; we only talked this one time. I politely listened

Sixty Single and Still Sizzling

to her conversation and ate the meal she prepared for us. I was happy, polite and respectful. After this encounter Johnathon had told me that she loved me and had enjoyed our conversation. 'She absolutely loves you,' he said. So, was he lying then or now? Who knows and in truth who cares? A lie is a lie. If she hated me now, she was as crazy as he was. I think she may have said that to mollify him. Mollifying a sixty-year-old man is slightly sickening.

After a difficult day, trying to keep focused on work and at the same time block online assaults, I returned home. Here I found all the personal possessions that I usually kept at his house, in a box on my back verandah. My jewellery was taped roughly to the door with silver Gaffa tape. In the box alongside my things were some of those that I had given him as gifts. A bit of selective rage here, I guess. Even a nail brush was returned. In hindsight I realised you can lead a horse to water and force him to drink but if he doesn't see the point, he will never drink by himself. I know that is a very mixed metaphor but it's how I see it. I pity his girlfriend if he has another relationship.

After this difficult and bewildering day, I messaged his daughter, the one I had got on well with, the nice one, and said I'm sorry you hate me but in truth I really liked you, and your dad is the one who caused the breakup in our relationship. She said she did not hate me at all, and her dad was lashing out as he always did when things did not go the way he perceived they should. It was not an uncommon occurrence.

So, another one had 'Bitten the Dust.' What a waste of time. Men can be sneaky; he should have told me of his depression issues. I had already spent years with a man who suffered from depression. It is not an easy walk for either partner. It was a difficult time for me. I would not have started the relationship with Johnathon if I had known he suffered from depression. This would have saved both a lot of hurt and confusion. One of his friends texted me a couple of weeks after we broke up asking me if I would reconsider my decision and give Johnathon another chance. I would not. Not now, maybe if we had communicated at the start of our relationship we could have talked through a lot of these issues before they became a flash point for him. The sad thing here is that his friends had known this would probably happen as it usually did but they had not shared that information with me.

This break up was a difficult one for me, I knew I could not go on with our relationship after this outburst of, what could only be described as an un-instigated, at least on my part, terrible rage. I had not seen this coming and was really upset and angry at the deceit and my own vulnerability.

People are difficult. I am not sure anymore if you can know anyone, especially if it is their intention for you not to know. If you cannot recognise mental instability and therefore be forewarned in five months of close contact, then how will you ever know if you are safe in any relationship.

People Who come and Go

For One Reason or Another.

I like to call Harry Foot Fetish Man.

Foot Fetish man loved my feet. I expect he loved lots of people's feet and mine were not the first to be lavished with his affection. After a few coffee dates he came to collect me from my home for a dinner date. He arrived for our date about fifteen minutes early with, 'a surprise,' for me. He had a bottle of wine, and he had a little black bag that he sat down on the chair beside us, he said, 'Let's have a wine and I'll give you a foot massage'. Who would ever refuse a foot massage? Certainly not me. Out comes all this pedicure stuff. Files and feet grinders, tow separators and polish. Massage oil and brushes. He pampered my feet for a long time. It was lovely but also a little weird. We eventually left for dinner, but I was quite curious as to what other little bags he had to 'pamper' me with. No, it was just a foot fetish thank goodness and he truly loved my feet. They often got more attention than the parts I would have preferred he gave attention to, but there was no harm in it, and I had the best manicured feet I'd ever had. We eventually drifted apart so I figure a prettier set of toes caught his eye and he couldn't resist the urge to pamper them.

Terry! I had been asked by a good friend to her 40th Wedding Anniversary at a lovely Swan Valley establishment. I was to be collected in the limousine with them as an honoured guest. I asked a gentleman that I had only dated a couple of times before to come along as my partner. He said he would love to come. Alarmingly when he hopped in the limo with the others his feet were sticking out in the middle, and he was wearing sneakers. Sneakers and a dress suit? I had told him the dress code and the venue. I believe there are celebrities and eccentrics who do this sort of down dressing style, but we were not rich and famous enough for that. He knew this was totally inappropriate. I asked him later if he did not have any other shoes, but his explanation was, he wanted to be comfortable. He said, 'They were black.' Fair enough. You have to laugh! I would have liked to have worn my Ugg boots.

Owen. I met Owen via a friend. 'I have a lovely cousin,' she said. 'He is here on a visit; would you like to meet him?' 'Why not.' I replied. He lived up to her description while he was in Western Australia but later when I visited him in his hometown it was evident that I was not going to be given the time or effort to make too much of a disturbance in his world. When he had visited, we got on well and it was understood that when I could go, I would go to spend some holiday time with him. Later that year he invited me to go to his home in another State. We were finally able to travel interstate and I felt like I would like to do just that. When I arrived, he was kind and attentive. As he lived in the Northern Beaches region of New South Wales, I flew into Brisbane airport. We went to a lovely restaurant on the ocean at the Gold Coast for lunch on the way home. I felt with such a delightful beginning it would be a fun two weeks. Well, it was fun, but this was despite Owen, who, after this initial effort to entertain me and spend time with me, left me to my own devices. I amused myself and spent most of the time alone.

Sixty Single and Still Sizzling

He gave me the car keys to the smallest car I have every driven and he would, here and there, ask me if I wanted any money. if I was going to go grocery shopping for the house, I would take his card but just as many times I took my own. He had been given a set of mosaic tools and kept them for me, this was thoughtful, and he created me a small workplace in the garage. I bought some mosaic cutters and thankfully for my sanity there was an awesome little mosaic tesserae store in town. I spent a lot of hours sitting at a small desk in the garage making mosaic. I could have done this at home, and I usually did.

Owen was not mean to me at all, but he was not available to me on what was meant to be a 'see how we get along,' type of visit. If I asked him for anything he would try to help. He cut some small boards for me so I could mosaic them, that sort of thing. I tried to engage in conversation with him, but he was working on a rebuild project on an old home. He went off to work early and came in about 4pm. He never actually came into the house he came into the garage in fact where he sat playing cards on his computer and consuming endless cans of beer until around 8pm when, already three stubbies short of a coma, he came in for dinner. For the first few days I thought he was still at work while all the time he was consuming beer at an alarming rate in the garage. I usually cooked dinner for us but not always. He did not demand anything or expect anything of me. He always wanted gravy. It was as if I was there and that was fine but if I wasn't, well that was fine too.

On the weekends he would take me out for a drive. He never got out of the car. We would drive as close as we could to some tourist attraction, and I had to look out through the car window. Of course, I was welcome to get out and do as I liked but he always waited patiently for me in the car. If I got out and had a look around it was always just me, by myself.

We went to a small coastal town to visit his family. We took a coaster bus and parked it in the yard. The home was in the middle of town, so it was easy to walk anywhere. I suggested we go out for breaky. To which he told me there was a great café just down the street. 'Cool lets go then.' I said. He answered, 'I'm not going to a café when we can go inside the house for breakfast.' He didn't add its free in there but that's what he meant. 'I would like to go out,' I say, 'Can you bring me a coffee?' he asks.

Nothing much was going well. I drove around the countryside and took daily trips here and there. I did a few sleepovers in small country towns for something to do. I thought this is not working out. There was nowhere we were amazingly compatible. Although Owen was keen on sex, which was amazing with all the beer he consumed, he was not particularly good in bed. He simply decided he would like sex and then would proceed to kiss me in his strange style, like pecking a child on the lips, but being careful to be chaste about it. This 'kissing' could lead to 'Goodnight' or it could lead to him going further and this without much introduction or, God forbid, any foreplay. I did my best to give him a chance, but conversation was lost on him, and he did not see the problem.

In his opinion he was fine in the sack, had been all his life. No other woman was complaining about his prowess, and he had had a few women since his divorce. I did say, 'maybe that's why they come and go,' but he would not have that. He was fine! He was also quite deaf and found wearing his hearing aids just too much trouble. I got sick of trying to talk, repeating every second word before giving up in frustration. He was a thin man, but he had a round tummy which sometimes pushed into me during cuddles, I would tell him to move as he was squashing me. He would not stop until I would just have to push him. We both always laughed at this. This craziness was mostly because of his deafness. I am glad I have a great sense of the ridiculous

Sixty Single and Still Sizzling

but after a few unsatisfactory nights in the bedroom, I decided to give up and go home.

When we first met, I had made it clear to him that I would not, under any circumstance, be prepared to move to interstate. I felt it was important that he know this in advance. He agreed and told me he had thought of moving to Western Australia anyway. Now, with the loneliness, the uncomfortable, and somewhat ridiculous sex and the looming closure of the Western Australian border, it was time to go home. It didn't take much effort to conclude that the idea, of there being an us in the equation, was a fantasy. I was pretty much by myself all the time. He was pulling back on the idea of moving to Western Australia, and in truth I just didn't like him that much anymore. As a partner there was nothing. As a friend there was some probability.

As you will know if you are a Western Australian, our border was very well protected during the covid years. I prepared to gather the necessary paperwork to return home and there were less and less planes available. It was becoming increasingly urgent to get home. I had the correct, approved paperwork a couple of times and was ready to go to the airport when my flight would be cancelled, or my approvals revoked due to outbreaks on the Gold Coast where I was flying from. I had to get a permit to get into QLD, so it was a bit touch and go. I experienced my first and thankfully only, panic attack during this period of time. I booked myself business class to avoid crowds on the plane and when I finally got to fly there were six of us on the plane and only me in business class. A big waste of money and time. But I finally got back to my home and two weeks of isolation.

Let's talk about Lionel. Lionel appeared to be nice. We have had long telephone conversations and now after about a month we were going to meet up. I broke my rule of waiting no longer than two weeks to catch up, this was due to the fact we lived a fair distance apart. He finally arrived in my hometown and at our first meeting all things were going along well, he made no assumptions, he said, and he had booked into a chalet for a few nights. Great, I liked this idea that there was no pressure to spend the nights together in my bed, I also noted that it was a lovely resort with a lovely big bed.

We spent a fun weekend together so I decided this would have to be the time when I told him that I have lied about my age on the dating site. I thought this was the right thing to do especially as we seemed to be getting on well and it appeared we really liked each other. So, the thought that our relationship may go on to being a long one I felt I must come clean. He said he had already worked that out but could not understand why I had made myself to be older as most people went the other way. At first, I thought he was joking as I had done as almost everyone else does and lowered my age somewhat. I reiterated that I was five years older than I had said on the site and in fact I was sixty-five. He kept saying, 'you're lying, and I can't work out the reason for this.' Eventually I told him, 'It's up to you to believe what you like.' He was teasing me later and I pointed out that on the site he had exaggerated his height, I knew this as I was taller than him. If he had been the height he had posted, I would have been a few inches shorter.

Lionel snored so loudly that even in the next room, with my earplugs in I could still hear every resonating sound. I was into my fourth night with very little sleep so I was in a very touchy mood, and it was on the cards that something would go wrong.

Eventually the time came when I had to go into work. Lionel was supposed to be staying only a few days but as we were getting on so well, he decided to extend his time with me. We were in an extremely busy period, and staff was in short supply because of the effects of covid 19 on the community, I had no option. I told Lionel that I had to go to work and would be back in a few hours but despite my saying,

Sixty Single and Still Sizzling

'I'll be back soon, get some rest and have a look around the area,' he insisted he wanted to come with me to help. He should have gone sightseeing or something like that. Maybe he could have gone and bought me flowers. But no, he wanted to stay with me. This turned out to be a disaster.

We had only just got inside the door of the busy gallery when he decided to tell me everything I was doing wrong, he could see it all in one second as he walked in to the building. This was despite him never running a business, let alone owning and managing one. He had spent his life as a combat soldier. I would have no concept of being a combat soldier and would never have assumed that I could know more than him of what went on in the day-to-day life of one. I had a humorous sign on my wall which said in bold letters, 'Be Nice or Get Out!' He found this to be outrageous and felt it would put off customers. I pointed out that if they wanted to be 'not nice' then I preferred them to go elsewhere. He told me I was foolish. He knew absolutely nothing of my business, whether it was successful or not. My customers loved the sign.

So, there we were in a busy café, customers were all over and I was trying to do my job with him following me all over and getting in the way of me and everyone else. The staff were frowning at him and wondering what was going on. Lionel was telling the Barista how to make the perfect expresso or something like that, while he was making long lists of coffee orders. To avoid an unpleasant scene in front of all my customers, who would absolutely love that to happen, this is a small town and almost anything is big news. I decided I would leave the shop and take Lionel with me.

Poor Lionel, who had now got himself into an argument on how to run the kitchen, didn't have a clue that he was on the edge of disaster. He reluctantly left with me as he was still convinced that he could be of help. He wanted to show me how to completely reorganise, make more money and basically do everything differently, right now. I explain that you can't change how we do things just like that or chaos will follow. He says, 'if you're the boss you can do as you like.' I answered very strongly, 'Yes I am the boss, and we are leaving now.'

Later that day I am being confronted by an angry man who tells me I am a bitch and I have an unhealthy relationship with my staff, particularly the Barista, because I let him push me around. I don't let anyone 'push me around' but coffee making is a serious business and the Barista was very busy. My business was successful because he is an amazing Barista. I wanted him to be able to do his job without interruptions. As for Lionel, I needed him to go home. I needed to sleep and sort out my emotions around him and his behaviour. I told him this and he agreed and left to return to his home. I thought this was a good idea. It would be good to have time out from each other, after all it had been a busy four days and maybe some time would give him perspective. At this point I was not thinking it was all over. I thought we had had a bit of a difference of opinion. I wasn't impressed at being called a bossy bitch but thought I could perhaps live with that. Later that day when he had arrived home, he sent me a vile text. I had to ask a girlfriend what some of it meant. She interpreted it to mean, when she broke it down, I was bossy, and I was a demanding and at the same time distracted lover. We were not sure of this description, but it wasn't too important to me, and I wasn't worried about it. We all want to be amazing in bed and have this acknowledged, but I was happy to see him out of my life so was not to upset. I know where the unhealthy relationship was, and it was not with the Barista. So, I was back to round one. I restarted the game.

A few months later Lionel contacted to me online, he had reinvented himself with a new username to get around the fact I have blocked him on several devices and on the online dating site where I met him. He asked me for forgiveness saying he didn't know what was wrong with him. I didn't tell him. I politely answered, 'of course you are forgiven but no, there is no chance of a catch up.' I had already moved on and I also know that leopard a will not change its spots so quickly. I did, however, ask him about the text, and his description of me and my lovemaking technique, this was of interest to me as I have the idea, I am an easy going, fun person in bed. He said he was an idiot and that he was just lashing out as things had not turned out how he had envisaged. It is important to not fall into the trap with anyone, in any life situation, where you are planning to change them. You can't change anyone else, but you can change yourself.

Murray. Murray contacted me via the online site while I was staying at a friend's beach house in the Midwest. I looked up his profile and he had a picture of himself with a big black cattleman's hat on. He was holding a rifle. He was a reasonable fit looking man, and I said 'hello,' back. A few days later I showed his picture to my friend and asked her who he looked like as it had been niggling at the back of my mind. Unfortunately for him, we realised it was a salubrious mass murderer. Even though this was a bit creepy I told myself to be sensible, you can't help who you look like, and that I should just see where our conversations led. We were living in towns about two hundred miles apart, so I asked to meet in the middle for a coffee which is my policy. Remember the rule to meet early if you possibly can and we could. This did not suit him, he wanted to talk on the phone for a few weeks to get to know me. I said, 'no this is not my way of going about things.' I said goodbye and was greeted with all sorts of abuse. Remember we had only spoken on the site; despite this he began to accuse me of all sorts of negative behaviour. I blocked him of course, but he continued to reinvent himself to find me. When I eventually met my Mr Right and left the site, he was still trolling me. I did report him but as I said before the sites appear not to care.

I was banned from being on the site at one time. I went to log in as usual and couldn't do so. I looked at my email and had received an email telling me I 'had used offensive pictures.' I had not done any such thing. The reason I am recalling all of this is that, rather than argue or try to get them to re-open my profile, I changed my site name and recreated my profile in minutes.

Covid man was a very unusual man. We were to meet for coffee. I was walking down the street toward a man who I thought was him, he saw me and came rushing up to me. He stopped a few feet away and began to address me in quite an aggressive manner. 'I hope you are not buying this covid crap. I'm not buying any of it. I won't be getting any vaccination; it's a government conspiracy and I'm not being forced into anything.' He went on and on until I, standing my three feet away, say, 'are you Harry?' 'Oh yes, I am,' he responds then continues his tirade. 'I'll have to go,' I say across the noise of his ranting and walk back to my car. I can certainly pick them.

Sometimes you can't see it coming then it is standing right in front of you. Madness! I dated a man for a few coffees and lunch at the pub, then he asked me to come to his farm to meet his dogs. A sort of, love me love my dogs, test. I agreed and showed up a few days later. The table was set for lunch and under our placemats were folded sheets of newspaper. I said 'what's with the fancy paper placemats?' He very seriously said it was in case we dropped crumbs. I was not impressed but chose to ignore this idiosyncrasy and went to sit on a chair in lounge. All the curtains were drawn, and it was dark. I went to open a curtain and was told very firmly, 'don't do that the garden is dying and I don't want to see it.' I was not keen on sitting in the dark, so we settled for lights. I ate my lunch, careful to not make any mess on anything, and headed off home very quickly. I liked the little dogs but him, no! And thus, another one went down the tube.

Sixty Single and Still Sizzling

Amongst my dating experiences were many that did not go past the first catch up, usually a coffee or tea in a small café somewhere out in the pubic. Many of these simply had misrepresented to the point that they were nothing like the person you thought you were catching up with. Some were rude. One horrid man pinched me on my nipple as I was getting into my car. Not what you do!

Some were simply unable to stop talking about themselves. But two who, in almost every other way, may have got past the first date made a constant slurping and swallowing noise. I didn't get what it was and why someone would make this noise. They both said sorry, 'hay fever,' but I didn't think so. I mentioned it to a friend saying it was a pity as I liked this guy, but the noise was off putting and annoying. She suggested loose dentures were the culprit. So, guys and gals if you have dentures make sure they fit properly.

I made lunch for a gentleman at my café and he simple could not stop eating. I thought this is ridiculous. I began to worry about stock levels!

Another I met up with for a lunch date. I thought he looked lovely. A great start as he looked like I had expected him to. However, my interest was short lived when in the early part of our date some friends of his came in and they proceeded to talk together until I just left and went back to work. He didn't notice.

Not every date led to another conversation. Most didn't. You instantaneously know if you like a person enough for another meet up. This goes for both people in the equation. Some Saturdays I would have a meeting with three or four potential Mr Rights. If you're getting dressed up, then why not. I sort out male advise on doing this and the necessity to tell each person you were catching up, or had caught up, with another man. This was a definitive, 'that's nobody's business but yours.'

One prospective Mr Right drove five hundred kilometres to catch up with me before I drove off to the airport for a two-week overseas break. He couldn't wait till I returned as he did not want to risk my meeting Mr Right on the trip. I said 'OKAY! if you really want to do this'. I thought it was silly and unnecessary as I was unlikely to meet anyone on the trip away with girlfriends, but he did it. He arrived at the venue where I was out with some friends to listen to music, and he got out of his car. He had texted me, so I met him outside. Security guards around so I was not concerned. I went to say, 'hello,' but he got back in his car, and said, 'you don't like me. I can tell by the look on your face'. I told him I thought he was being hasty and should at least have a coffee before leaving but he announced he could see the disappointment in my eyes. He turned the car around and headed out of town. I was unable to explain his behaviour and I never heard from him again. Weeks later when recalling the incident, I realised he looked a lot like a man from my very distant past that I had little time for. Maybe I reflected this distaste. Or maybe he did not like the look of me.

In this group of first dates there were also some men who did not think I was the one for them, I am a happy, confident, self-reliant woman and I know I am not everyone's cup of tea.

Getting Things Mixed up.

It was Bound to Happen

Remember back at the start of this book I said you must be careful not to confuse one man with a different man. There was a situation where I did just that. I had a habit of putting the names of men I was conversing with into my phone with the name of the town or city they were from as their surname. I had talked on the online site, and a few times, by phone with a man from a certain country town. During one of these conversations, he told me he liked to do his farm work naked, and I needed to be aware of this if we got together. I needed to be comfortable with nudity. He also told me his appetite for sex was excessive and after a bit of thought I took the hint that he was trying to give me reason to go away without him having to say tell me he wasn't interested. We stopped talking and went our different ways. I am telling you this as it got be a bit mixed up later down the track.

About five months later I met a man, let's call him Les, we met up in a small town not far from where he lived. He happened to live in the same town as the first man did. I recorded them both in my phone with the same last name, the name of the town. On the phone he seemed kind and he was good to talk to, so I was happy to go out of my way to meet him on a drive down to Perth. When I saw him walking toward me I noticed he was a big man and he seemed unable to bend his legs. He had hair coming out of his nose and on top of his nose in copious amounts. I wondered how he breathed. His ears had spikes of hair coming out and his eyebrows put a Muppet to shame. EEK. Well as I am a nice girl, and I was hungry, we had lunch together. I was mesmerised with the hair everywhere and it was hard to keep track of our conversation. I didn't mind in fact because I was already strongly convinced, I would not see this man again. When we left to go to our cars, he said goodbye and that maybe we would meet again. I smiled and began to drive off. He held his hand to stop me from driving away and came over to the car. 'You are clean and tidy, aren't you?' He asked. I was a bit taken back. I stopped and looked at him. I assumed that he must be talking about my home life as right now, at our lunch meeting I was presenting as a very clean, tidy, well-dressed woman. I cannot tell you how annoyed I was by this question. How rude! When had he looked in a mirror? If I was tidying anything up it would be his facial hair, and I'm not talking about his beard. Did he think I was going to be his maid. Anyway, I answered, 'Definitely not. You will have to employ a cleaner if we get together.' When someone's only concern after meeting you once is your ability to clean, then I think you have a problem. He is looking for a housekeeper not a wife.

 Now here is where I got myself confused as in my phone he was stored as Les Certain Country Town. I think he had given some thought to the fact I was not going to clean for him and later during that week, he sent me a text message saying he would be busy for a while and would contact me later when he could. Me, thinking he was the first man from this town answered, 'please don't do that, I am not up for being chased naked around the apple trees by a sex crazed man,'

Needless to say, and thankfully, I never heard from hairy man again. I never heard from the naked, tree skipping, man, again either.

Mr Right

The Story of You.
My last few months online had produced the same as had the few months before that. I felt that it was not possible to find the 'Man' I was looking for. The space was too wide and vast. I had decided to give up. If Mr Right was out there, he needed to be searching harder for me.

I had come home from the Kimberley for the four-day Christmas break. My daughter asked if I was seeing anyone or had met any fun people online. I told her I had given up, even though I had used a paid site last time and one for older singles, everyone was the same. I had used the paid site, with the idea that if people were prepared to pay to connect, they may be more serious and may indeed be a better quality of contact. This was not the case. Even though a lot of people say they are looking for a 'long term relationship' that's not what they want, they want you to be available to them for a long time. Their idea of the long-time part is that you stay in your space, and they'll stay in theirs. We'll meet in the middle when we need something from each other.

This was not for me. I wanted the real thing. I wanted to be in love with someone. I wanted to feel my spirits lift when I heard a certain voice or saw your face. I wanted to be loved and to love in return. I knew that I would give up some freedoms for this, but I was happy to do that. I knew what I wanted and settling for anything less was not for me. Living alone is not terrible, in many ways freedom is wonderful. You must receive more, from any relationship, than you lose by giving up your freedom.

'Don't give up' she said, 'look at how me and Justin met,' Sceptically and somewhat reluctantly I agreed to keep trying, for at least the last three months of my paid-up subscription. She had not been on a dating site but had met via a friendship group so I took her point that life and love can change in an instant.

Now a few months before this I was having lunch by myself down at the beach when I met a gentleman, the meeting was quite by chance. We were eating at neighbouring tables and holding a general conversation across the intervening space, 'Shall I join you?' he asked, 'Sure,' I said. We were talking about finding our perfect match and the improbability of that being possible. He felt that many people don't get what they want because they have not clearly defined what that is. Not even to themselves. He was a traveller and was on his third trip around Australia. He was travelling in a motor home and was enjoying the lifestyle, not really wanting to settle down.

He had been successful in helping his niece find her true love and life companion by showing her how to use the visualization method of attracting what, or in this case who, you want. I am a firm believer in the visualisation method of attraction and had for a few months now been visualising my new home, I had pictures and descriptions on my wall which I looked at and read through every morning. I just hadn't considered the concept with a person. Later in the day I realised that I too had not clearly defined my perfect partner and was sort of hoping I would know him when I met him. I was looking for someone, but I had no real idea of what would make him Mr Right and thus Perfect for me. I felt there was nothing to lose, and I decided to give it a go and that night I wrote out my 'perfect man' scenario.

I sent this wish through to my new friend via a long text message and he wrote back and said to rewrite it all, looking back from twenty years in the future. I laughed at this because twenty years was a bit ambitious at my age but thought, why not.

He also suggested I use only positives in the description. An example of this was, instead of writing 'No Smoking,' write, 'It is wonderful he doesn't smoke.' I rewrote the description of my perfect man, my Mr Right.

I read this description of my wonderful partner every morning. I read it aloud along with the one regarding my new home. I had the handwritten descriptions of them both stuck on the wall in my kitchen where I saw them each morning. I read them out loud. I did not want to forget.

Here is the final draft of my wants, needs and desires in the man who would be perfect for me. I wrote this six months before I met Jack.

MY VISUALIZATION STATEMENT.

I love my partner. He is kind.
He never raises his voice in anger.
He is healthy and fit.
He communicates well.
We enjoy outings and staying at home together.
He embraces my family.
He is not a smoker.
He drinks moderately.
He has enough money to live well with me.
We travel together.
He enjoys live music.
He enjoys sex and is a considerate lover.
He loves to spend most of his time with me but has interests of his own that I am not involved in.

Sixty Single and Still Sizzling

I thought I would give dating on the online sites a few more months especially, as I said before I had a few more months on my subscription. I decided I would be extremely specific in who I was looking for. After all I now knew who I was searching for. Mr Right had been defined!

I did not rely on just dating sites and spent time and effort in getting out and about even when I had to go by myself. This was often and I enjoyed my own company. Sometimes I would share a table with another party, with another person, male and female, or group and I met some interesting folks this way. A lot of people travel for work, and they are alone so someone to chat with is great.

I was now working on a short-term work contract in the Kimberley region of Western Australia. I was a long way from anywhere. Anything could happen.

In January of 2022 I connected with a gentleman online. He was, as his profile said, a farmer, a widow and was looking for a lady to be part of his life. He was also smiling in his profile picture, and he looked a very soft and gentle person. Smiling in his profile picture was an immediate draw as I said earlier almost no man has a smiling picture. He was the same age as me and I had to take into considerations that most men I had previously met in this age group were totally not suited to me. He was, however, saying all the right things and he was smiling. I thought that, despite his age, he sounded perfect for me. At the same time, I was feeling that the distance between us may make a relationship impossible and so it may not be worthwhile saying hello. He lived South of Perth, many long miles away from my Kimberley adventure.

However, fate intervened in my procrastinations when he said hello to me, and we began an online conversation, which, within a few days, changed to a telephone conversation. During these early conversations he never once asked me what colour undies I was wearing.

Usually the leading question after hello. Rarely answered and usually the end of the call. This was a pleasant side to Jack, and I appreciated it very much. We would talk for hours every day. Working up north was a lonely time for me, and I looked forward to these calls. I was returning to Perth in February for a concert so he and I decided we should meet up at that time. We both knew that it was time to get together. I know I broke my two-week rule, but you can see that it was an unrealistic rule in the circumstances. Despite all of this I kept all my private information to myself, and we discussed travel, farming, life and death, all the easy stuff.

I arrived in Perth in February as I was booked for the Boyup Brook Country Music festival. This is a weekend I love. I usually go by myself as not many of my friends, especially the women, will admit they love country. Often, once there, I will meet up with people I know already, it's a great fun weekend.

Again, fate was pushing us closer together, as this year, once again the festival was cancelled due to a last-minute attempt by the Covid 19 virus to cause us all more disappointment and rule our lives, and I now had two weeks with not a lot on the schedule.

So, the day after I arrived in the city, we met for lunch as planned, what followed was the perfect day. Of course, saying, 'we met for lunch,' is a very simplistic version of the planning, pampering and anticipation I went through. Eventually I settled for a sun dress and sandals, along the, less is more line of thinking. I am not sure how I would have dealt with my feelings if he had not been the gorgeous man he still is. Jack picked me up from where I was staying as I did not have my car. Lunch was long and relaxed at one of my favourite city restaurants along the northern beaches. We talked for hours over lunch and coffee, neither of us wanting to end the day. We finished the lunch with a walk along the beach. Jack was wearing RM Williams boots which I found strangely attractive for some reason.

Sixty Single and Still Sizzling

The boots got wet, and he did not care. No, he would not take his shoes off. His feet would get sandy, and he had to head home soon. He was a farmer so was preparing for seeding at the time. I did not know how much I was distracting him from his day-to-day work, but I knew I really liked him.

When he drove me back to where I was staying, we were saying goodbye and I leaned across and kissed him. A gentle friendly kiss to let him know I thought he was delicious. He was responsive and returned my kiss. Still a gentle, but more romantic, kiss. He had not hesitated. I enjoyed the interaction and said so, he said. 'Yes!' That's all he said! Reluctantly we parted, after making plans for me to visit him at his home on my way back from visiting my children further south. I was looking forward to going to his farm and spending more time with him.

I had a great visit with my family, but my mind was elsewhere, and I thought of Jack a lot in that week. I was a little nervous when arriving at the farmhouse. It was a lovely home with wide verandahs all the way around the house. It looked exactly like the home I had been visualising for many months only the verandahs were much bigger.

Jack was a perfect gentleman. He had prepared all sorts of little things to make me comfortable, from wine and chocolates to bath products. Jack had a little dog that was quite aggressive in telling me that Jack was his and I should leave now. I ignored him knowing he would be eating out of my hands in a few days. I like dogs and they like me.

Jack spent time showing me around the house and talking about the farm and what he was growing. We got to the bedrooms and Jack showed me he had made up the spare room for me, he had it looking lovely, and I thought, 'what a shame,' as I had no intention of sleeping in there. Of course, this was my side of the equation and had he not been ready for me in his bed I would have been comfortable to use the spare room. When we got to his room I asked, 'am I not allowed to sleep in here with you?' He laughed and said, 'of course, you can, I hoped you would, but I was not going to make assumptions on that and scare you off.' What a sweetheart. Later I learned I had to share the bed with the little dog as well but he was quite small and didn't bother me too much so that was fine. Little dog and I take all our naps together these days.

Sadly, I had to go back to work, back to the Kimberley, but we planned for Jack to visit with me in about two weeks' time. It seemed to take forever but eventually he arrived. Once again, we felt wonderful together and like we had been with each other for years. When he returned to Perth, I was unhappy and found working depressing, so I decided to come back down to Perth. I knew that our chances at a successful relationship were diminished by the distance between us and as I had already fulfilled my original contract there was nothing holding me in the Kimberley. When I returned south Jack collected me at the airport and took me back to his home where I was planning to stay for a few weeks and then return to my home. When I told this plan to Jack, he asked me, 'why do that? Why don't you just stay here with me?' I was really happy with this idea, and I agreed as going back home to an empty house did not have any appeal to me. I wanted to stay here with him. So that is what I did, and I have been with him ever since.

Jack has been a lovely man and companion; he has to work so I do still spend time alone. He created a studio for me in the large conglomeration of sheds we had on the property, and it is the best workspace I have ever had to work in.

We've done a road trip together without one word of angst and I still find it hard to understand how I found him. It was sometime after I moved to his home, I realised he fulfilled all the requirements of my 'wish list,' and amazingly enough the house he was living in filled a whole lot of my perfect house desires. Especially the verandahs. I had always wanted a home with big verandahs and his had 4.2metre wide ones all the way around the house.

    I have asked Jack about his side of our connection, and he has shared the following thoughts with me. Jack was nervous but trying to reassure himself with the fact we had had countless conversations and he felt he knew me somewhat. He found me attractive, but he was still a bit concerned because of scammers and crazy women he had met previously. He knew looks were not everything. He says our lunch was the longest he had ever had, and he had enjoyed every minute of it. While lunch was a 'bit of blur,' he had really had a fun relaxing time. He thought I talked a lot but put that down to nerves. He has since learned that it wasn't nerves and I do talk a lot. Jack was keen to see me again. He was very impatient with the time we were apart. He is glad he found me.

    As for me I'm glad we found each other, Jack is sort of like an old pair of slippers that you find at the back of your wardrobe. They fit you perfectly and are very comfortable. You never want to take them off.

Conclusion.

Nearly Two Years of Being in Love and Being Loved

Its more than two years since our first conversation. We have moved house and bought a new one together. He is my perfect match. I get all the attention I need but he is no push over. We have long and in-depth conversation about just about everything. I am now an expert on planting canola and caring for a crop. We have not, yet, sat down to watch the Hobbit movies together but he does enjoy fantasy and we do watch a lot of that, usually with a wine and not a cocoa but it is close enough for me. Little dog loves me very much. He searches around for me if I'm away from home and loves to have a cuddle from me. He is still Jack's dog though. Nothing is going to change that.

Right now, Jack and I and little dog are undertaking an around Australia trip, we are seven weeks in and have forty-five weeks to go. We are planning to return at the end of the year, but it can be extended if we find ourselves wanting to explore more. Maybe we will see you along the way.

I feel blessed to have met Jack, but I also am aware I did put a lot of time and energy and determination into the search for him. I refused to give in, and I was encouraged by friends but mostly family to keep going when I wanted to quit and come and live with them. Just kidding. I believe the universal energies responded to me and brought us together. If they can do this for us, then they can do it for you. Don't give up. Don't settle and it will happen. And if it doesn't you will have at least had an entertaining and sometimes hilarious adventure along the way.

Be safe!

Dating Worksheet

My Rules

Sixty Single and Still Sizzling

Dawn La Puma

Sixty Single and Still Sizzling

Do's and Don'ts

Sixty Single and Still Sizzling

Dawn La Puma

Sixty Single and Still Sizzling

Dates and stories. What worked for me What didn't.

Sixty Single and Still Sizzling

Dawn La Puma

Sixty Single and Still Sizzling

Dawn La Puma

Names Address telephone Nos.

Sixty Single and Still Sizzling

Dawn La Puma

Sixty Single and Still Sizzling

Sensitive Information.

Sixty Single and Still Sizzling

Dawn La Puma

Sixty Single and Still Sizzling

Notes in case you too decide to write your memoirs.

Sixty Single and Still Sizzling

Dawn La Puma

Sixty Single and Still Sizzling

Dawn La Puma

Sixty Single and Still Sizzling

Dawn La Puma

Sixty Single and Still Sizzling

www.ingramcontent.com/pod-product-compliance
Lightning Source LLC
Chambersburg PA
CBHW051451290426
44109CB00016B/1704